NEW ESSAYS ON THE AMERICAN

★ The American Novel ★

GENERAL EDITOR

Emory Elliott, Princeton University

Other books in the series:
New Essays on The Scarlet Letter
New Essays on The Great Gatsby
New Essays on Adventures of Huckleberry Finn
New Essays on Moby-Dick
New Essays on Uncle Tom's Cabin
New Essays on The Red Badge of Courage
New Essays on Light in August
New Essays on The Sun Also Rises

Forthcoming:
New Essays on Chopin's The Awakening (ed. Wendy Martin)
New Essays on Ellison's Invisible Man (ed. Robert O'Meally)

New Essays on
The American

Edited by

Martha Banta

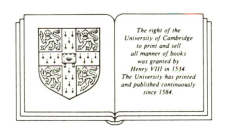

The right of the
University of Cambridge
to print and sell
all manner of books
was granted by
Henry VIII in 1534.
The University has printed
and published continuously
since 1584.

CAMBRIDGE UNIVERSITY PRESS

Cambridge

New York   New Rochelle   Melbourne   Sydney

Published by the Press Syndicate of the University of Cambridge
The Pitt Building, Trumpington Street, Cambridge CB2 1RP
32 East 57th Street, New York, NY 10022, USA
10 Stamford Road, Oakleigh, Melbourne 3166, Australia

First published 1987

Printed in the United States of America

Library of Congress Cataloging-in-Publication Data
New essays on The American.
(The American novel)
Bibliography: p.
1. James, Henry, 1843–1916. American. I. Banta,
Martha. II. Series.
PS2116.A63N48   1987   813'.4   86-33405
ISBN 0 521 30730 9 hard covers
ISBN 0 521 31449 6 paperback

British Library Cataloging-in-Publication data applied for.

Contents

Contents

5
Physical Capital: *The American*
and the Realist Body
MARK SELTZER
page 131

Series Editor's Preface

In literary criticism the last twenty-five years have been particularly fruitful. Since the rise of the New Criticism in the 1950s, which focused attention of critics and readers upon the text itself – apart from history, biography, and society – there has emerged a wide variety of critical methods which have brought to literary works a rich diversity of perspectives: social, historical, political, psychological, economic, ideological, and philosophical. While attention to the text itself, as taught by the New Critics, remains at the core of contemporary interpretation, the widely shared assumption that works of art generate many different kinds of interpretation has opened up possibilities for new readings and new meanings.

Before this critical revolution, many American novels had come to be taken for granted by earlier generations of readers as having an established set of recognized interpretations. There was a sense among many students that the canon was established and that the larger thematic and interpretative issues had been decided. The task of the new reader was to examine the ways in which elements such as structure, style, and imagery contributed to each novel's acknowledged purpose. But recent criticism has brought these old assumptions into question and has thereby generated a wide variety of original, and often quite surprising, interpretations of the classics, as well as of rediscovered novels such as Kate Chopin's *The Awakening,* which has only recently entered the canon of works that scholars and critics study and that teachers assign their students.

The aim of The American Novel Series is to provide students of American literature and culture with introductory critical guides to

American novels now widely read and studied. Each volume is devoted to a single novel and begins with an introduction by the volume editor, a distinguished authority on the text. The introduction presents details of the novel's composition, publication history, and contemporary reception, as well as a survey of the major critical trends and readings from first publication to the present. This overview is followed by four or five original essays, specifically commissioned from senior scholars of established reputation and from outstanding younger critics. Each essay presents a distinct point of view, and together they constitute a forum of interpretative methods and of the best contemporary ideas on each text.

It is our hope that these volumes will convey the vitality of current critical work in American literature, generate new insights and excitement for students of the American novel, and inspire new respect for and new perspectives upon these major literary texts.

Emory Elliott
Princeton University

1

Introduction

MARTHA BANTA

W HEN Henry James began work on *The American* in
1875, he was impelled by three interconnected needs, all to
do with finding the "right forms." He had to give shape to his
nascent career by driving it forward in the direction that would
best enhance his reputation as a promising young writer; he had to
decide what authorial perspective to take on the material he treated in his narrative and whether to guide it toward the literary
genre of the romance (locus of the fanciful) or the novel (seat of
the realist); he had to define to his own satisfaction what the
American character was in relation, first, to the United States,
which he perceived as essentially formless, and, second, to a foreign culture whose historical forms were all too rigidly in place.

It was mid-1876 by the time James completed his story of
Christopher Newman, the freewheeling American millionaire
abroad in the Paris where James had felt himself at odds. While
James was busy raising questions about where habits of independence and self-reliance got a man like Newman and pursuing his
unofficial exposition of the meaning of "the American," his compatriots were gathering back home in Philadelphia to celebrate the
one-hundredth anniversary of the nation's severance from the Old
World in 1776. Many were responding with patriotic pride to the
lavishly stocked exhibition halls of the 1876 centennial, which
appeared to give credence to the belief that the United States had
come very far very fast over the past century – as a growing
political power, as the catalyst for astonishing technological
achievements, and as the champion of a democratic culture. The
good people across the ocean from James were flushed with self-
congratulation as they passed through the official displays, finding

there affirmation of the national unity they liked to think that the North had snatched from the jaws of hell during the Civil War concluded ten years earlier. The American types described in the news media of the day were pleased to observe that the overt making of big wars had been replaced by the making and spending of big money and the enhancement of a peaceful, prosperous, and virtuous society.

In order for such assertions of national pride to be made, blind eyes had to be turned upon the kinds of warfare still in evidence from coast to coast: in the Reconstruction South, where newly emancipated blacks struggled to hold on to their meager gains in civil affairs in spite of the ominous light cast on the night skies by burning crosses lit by the Ku Klux Klan; in the western territories, where sweeps against the resisting Indian tribes were made (not always successfully, as General George Custer's debacle at Little Big Horn demonstrated) by army troops ordered to free the lands for white development; in the ornate boardrooms and smoky back rooms of the eastern power brokers, whose self-interested manipulations of the Crédit Mobilier and the Tweed Ring stole large sums of money from the shareholders of the Union Pacific Railroad and the treasury of New York City; in the railroad yards and coal mines banding the industrial states on the eve of the bloody strikes that would warn of anarchic social elements on the loose; in the silver fields of Nevada, where the excitement of flush times was followed by overnight busts and panics, both financial and psychological. Yes, on the American side of the Atlantic, the citizenry had either to acknowledge or to ignore the fact that it was well-nigh impossible to bring the official images of the progressive, unified, contented American character endorsed by the Philadelphia centennial to line with the ever-present expressions – sometimes violent, usually disquieting – of the random nature of American life.

Removed from these battlefronts back in the United States as he may have been, James's multifold search for necessary forms deeply involved him in his own campaign to wrest order out of confusion. At the same time, he needed to advance his career as a writer by selecting the fictional form that would satisfy his readers as well as the high literary standards he had already set for himself.

2

To bring about this double coup, James also had to push ahead with what turned out to be his lifelong search to determine what it means to be an American writing about the primary American types. By being alert to the aims and accomplishments of this thirty-two-year-old writer, we gain a history that places *The American* within its cultural and social context and in relation to the arc of James's development as a major American author.

1

In 1875 Henry James was in Paris and on his own. At thirty-two he was no longer the Small Boy later portrayed in the first volume of his memoirs as one who had been trundled about Europe during the 1840s and 1850s; he was no longer the direct object of his father's well-intentioned but whimsical experiments in an education that was meant to be vague enough to protect the five James children from achieving any kind of conventional success. James in 1875 was still, however, the junior Henry James and would sign himself thus until his father's death in 1883. He was still tied to the strings of a parental allowance that allowed his nature insufficient economic and emotional play. He could not call himself his own man until he attained the full financial independence that would come about only when his writings supported him entirely.

James had been a practicing writer since 1864. Over the next eleven years he produced a series of literary reviews, the fictional romances that appeared in 1875 under the collective title of *A Passionate Pilgrim and Other Tales,* and the travel pieces (also published in 1875) published as *Transatlantic Sketches*. His first big work – the novel *Roderick Hudson*, which he had commenced in Florence in 1873 and completed at his parents' home in Cambridge, Massachusetts, during the winter of 1874–5 – was appearing in the *Atlantic Monthly* as a serial at the time he recrossed the ocean to arrive in Paris in November 1875 – returning, in fact, to Europe for good. He had chosen his special vocation in 1864; now he chose the continent where he must manifest his fate as an American writer living abroad. "My choice is the old world – my choice, my need, my life," he wrote in his notebooks of 1881. "God knows that I have now no time to waste," he was still cautioning himself six years after that disembarkment of November 1875, as he would continue to admonish himself until his death in 1916.[1]

The pressures upon James to make his literary mark must have seemed especially arduous in 1875. Active as he had been in producing his reviews, travel sketches, apprentice tales, and first novel, he knew he could not pause for a moment if he were to keep himself financially afloat. Before coming to France he had made arrangements with Whitelaw Reid of the *New York Tribune* to contribute a series of letters appraising the Parisian scene, but he was gently released from his assignment by the summer of 1876 after twenty letters and payments from Reid amounting to $400. His reports on Paris, couched in the descriptive style he had developed for his earlier magazine pieces, proved unsuitable for the *Tribune*'s journalistic needs. He had not yet found the form appropriate for audiences other than those of *The Nation* and the *Atlantic Monthly*, with which he was familiar. James had never thought to place all of his professional eggs in Reid's basket, however. He was in Paris not three weeks when he sent a letter to F. P. Church, the editor of *The Galaxy*, proposing a novel-length serial under the title of *The American*. When *The Galaxy* did not respond to his suggestion, he immediately entered into a contractual agreement with William Dean Howells, editor of the *Atlantic Monthly*. Howells eagerly cleared the way for his magazine to receive the rights to the story James had momentarily laid aside as the result of the disappointing silence on the part of *The Galaxy*.[2]

James had been chastened and depressed by a letter of January 1876 from his mother that called him to task for his "extravagance" and the financial drain he was causing his father, in spite of the fact that he had sent the $200 derived from the sale of *Transatlantic Sketches* directly home to Cambridge. James's response had been to press ahead to deliver two short romances, "Crawford's Consistency" and "The Ghostly Rental," to *Scribner's Magazine* for a fee of $300. It was a great relief to him, therefore, to settle with Howells on the placement of *The American*, even though he was still far short of its completion when it first began to appear in the *Atlantic Monthly* in June 1876.

Though *The American* would run for twelve months and fetch

4

James $1,350 – enough to support him through 1876 – Leon Edel's biography details his continuing scramble during 1877; working at an accelerated pace, he produced ten essays for *The Galaxy,* three for *Lippincott's,* and still others for *The Nation* after his move to London at the end of 1876.[3] In the meantime, James was seeing *The American* through its *Atlantic Monthly* serialization and its first publication as a book in April 1877 under the imprint of James R. Osgood of Boston. Like most authors in the days before the international copyright law went into effect in 1891, James had to stand by without legal recourse as unauthorized editions appeared in London in 1877 and Germany in 1877 and 1878. An authorized London edition (slightly altered from the Osgood text) was published by Macmillan in 1879, followed later by the inclusion of *The American* in Macmillan's collection of James's novels in 1883. The final appearance of the novel during James's lifetime came in 1907, featured as the second volume of Scribners New York Edition of James's major works.[4] The consequences of *that* edition – heavily revised by James in 1905 – are a story in itself and one that will be treated later in this introduction, as will the implications of James's conversion of the novel into a stage play in 1892 for the controversies that followed the compositional evolution of Christopher Newman's story.

While James was in Paris commencing work on *The American,* he had more on his mind than the very real need to ensure his financial stability and to place his writings before the public in short order. He was in the midst of an evaluation of the general relation of Americans to French culture and an assessment of the significance to his own art of the Parisian literary scene represented by Gustave Flaubert, Alphonse Daudet, Émile Zola, Edmond de Goncourt, and Guy de Maupassant, as well as by Ivan Turgenev, the visiting Russian; he was also absorbing the lessons afforded by the nighttime spectacles of the Paris theater, which, some suggest, directly influenced the plot of *The American* and certainly lay behind the choices he later made in the development of his "scenic" art.[5]

In the end, Honoré de Balzac proved to be James's man rather than Flaubert or Maupassant; and also Turgenev, the writer who led James to commit himself to what one critic calls "that humanist-aesthetic cosmopolitanism, that freedom from 'our Anglo-Sax-on, Protestant, conventional morality' which he had so admired in Turgenev."[6] Incidentally, it was Turgenev who had first intro-duced James to Flaubert in December 1875, but by May 1876 James was writing Howells about his withdrawal from the group of French writers. "I have seen almost nothing of the literary fraternity, and there are fifty reasons why I should not become intimate with them. I don't like their wares, and they don't like any others; and besides, they are not *accuelillants.* Turgenev is worth the whole heap of them."[7] The casual immorality condoned by the Flaubertian circle, the petty animosities of its members toward those who did not fully concur with their methods, the enginelike way in which they produced volumes of "limited per-fection," and the seeming coldness and deadness of their hearts repelled James. The broad expansiveness of spirit he had found in Balzac's and Turgenev's writings was what James now realized he was after. *Cosmopolitanism,* in short.

What an odd position James found himself in, therefore, during the twelve months he spent in Paris delving deeper into his story of the American abroad. "I am turning into an old, and very con-tented Parisian," he informed Howells in a letter of May 1876.[8] "I feel as if I had struck roots into the Parisian soil, and were likely to let them grow tangled and tenacious there." Yet, he admitted, "Of pure Parisianism I see absolutely nothing." At the time, when expressing his feelings to Howells, James put a good face on the fact that he had no accepted place in French society and had denied himself the possibility of becoming allied with the newest French literary camp. Simply to be in Paris gave cheer, he asserted; Paris assured "that one can arrange one's life here exactly as one pleases – that there are facilities for every kind of habit and taste, and that everything is accepted and understood." This acute ob-server of the city's spectacle appreciated the fact that Paris was "a sort of painted background which keeps shifting and changing, and which is always there, to be looked at when you please, and to be most easily and comfortably ignored when you don't."

In 1875–6 James could liken himself to a member of a great audience enjoying the theatricality the city so brilliantly provided, but looking back from the vantage point of 1881, he admitted in the privacy of his notebooks that he had not much cared for the sense of estrangement he had experienced five years before.[9] Alone, because distanced from the parochialism of the French scene; alone, because he claimed no entrée into the French social world; alone, because as an American abroad he had to depend upon "the little American 'set' – the American village encamped *en plein Paris.*" James admitted that his compatriots "knew up to a certain point their Paris," but he judged their existence there to be "ineffably tiresome and unprofitable." He was constantly beset by the type of American woman whom he was to represent (somewhat more sympathetically) as Mrs. Tristram in *The American:* the kind who took upon herself "the right to judge" his movements. James felt trapped by "the detestable *American* Paris." He could not possess the French Paris, and he was increasingly annoyed by those Americans who tried to possess him as part of "their Paris." Realizing, "moreover, that I should be an eternal outsider," he decided "to abandon my plans of indefinite residence, take flight to London and settle there as best I could." So James departed for England in November 1876, one year after his arrival in Paris. Even though the early chapters of *The American* had already began to appear in the *Atlantic Monthly* in June 1876, the final portions of the story were still unfinished when he crossed the English Channel. Indeed, James was still corresponding with Howells concerning the developments of the narrative through March 1877.

The twelve months that had launched the story of Christopher Newman's confrontation with the "walls" of Parisian society marked a difficult period during which James himself had had to come to terms with those elements – internal as well as external – that seemed to prevent him from becoming the cosmopolitan man he urgently desired to be. Still, he had made several important discoveries: The parochialism he detested characterized the French literary clique as well as the tight little world of "the American 'set'"; this same incapacity for cultural and personal breadth also existed, he would argue in *The American,* within the well-guarded minds and imprisoned lives of the aristocratic French society represented by the Bellegarde family.

Certain of the literary problems James had in forming his portrayal of Americans in relation to Parisian life arose from the fact that he had had to solve the "money question" by hurrying his story into print "somewhat prematurely" while still in the process of undergoing, in his own experience, the several stages of initiation thrust upon his fictional hero.[10] The occasional weaknesses that marred the narrative as the result of James's failure to allow sufficient time to elapse before recollecting his Parisian impressions are offset by the stimulation to his imagination that came from his constantly having had to ask himself on the spot – *really* ask himself – what does it mean to be an American?

2

It is significant that Constance Rourke, who offered one of the first effective critical interpretations of *The American,* singled out James's novel for its portrayal of "a whole society of typical individuals." Rourke's watershed study of 1931, *American Humor,* is subtitled "A Study of the National Character." With this topic as her announced concern, it was right and fit that Rourke devoted an important segment of her book to the success of James's treatment of the consummate type of the Yankee and to the power of "the complete fable" he provided in the figure of Christopher Newman.[11]

The notion that one can "know" the qualities of a nation by knowing the character classification of its citizenry is as old as the notion of nationalism. Even older (as ancient as the writings of the Greek physiognomists) is the conviction that it is advantageous to study the general type rather than the particulars of random individuals; or rather, the conviction that such individuals come into sharp focus when grouped according to classified social types. The conceptual trajectory between Theophrastus and the "character books" of the seventeenth century, and on to Royall Tyler's *The Contrast* of 1787, is strong and clear. The distance from Tyler's comedy of manners, which pits the decent, unaffected, "natural" American against the hypocritical, pretentious fops of the Old World, to Christopher Newman confronting the arrogant, affected, moral decadents at the Bellegarde's Paris soiree is no distance at all.

Daisy Miller, the American Girl, together with her vague mother and her brother Randolph, with his brattish ways and sugar-rotted teeth, would emerge from James's imagination in 1879. Yankees beset by overnight wealth and uncertain taste stretched their long legs on the verandas of the resort hotels of Saratoga Springs in a piece he wrote for *The Nation* in 1870. Reticent New Englanders were set next to European sophisticates in his 1878 novel *The Europeans*, and 1881 found James cataloging an array of national types in *The Portrait of a Lady*. James had entered this important phase of his unfolding career by placing conscious emphasis upon the typical characteristics of his native Americans in contrast to, and in contest with, the European types he threw across their paths.

The opening pages of *The American* show James eying Newman's Lincolnesque physiognomy as intently as ever Melville examined the brow of Moby-Dick or as Hawthorne pored over Hester Prynne's scarlet **A**, but Melville's allegories of cosmic meaning and Hawthorne's symbols of humankind's complicity with sin and suffering are replaced on James's pages by the worldly immediacy of an observer with "an eye for national types."[12] This observer, in the narrator's words,

> would have had no difficulty in determining the local origin of this undeveloped connoisseur, and indeed such an observer might have felt a certain humorous relish of the almost ideal completeness with which he filled out the national mould. The gentleman on the divan was a powerful specimen of an American. But he was not only a fine American; he was in the first place, physically, a fine man. (pp. 17–18)

At this point, sounding for all the world like the plethora of physiognomical manuals produced for a public with a marked taste for the classification of skulls, noses, and jawbones, James details the way Newman appears to the world:

> He had a very well-formed head, with a shapely, symmetrical balance of the frontal and the occipital development, and a good deal of straight, rather dry brown hair. His complexion was brown, and his nose had a bold, well-marked arch. His eye was of a clear, cold gray, and save for a rather abundant moustache, he was clean-shaved. He had the flat jaw and sinewy neck which are frequent in

the American type; but the traces of national origin are a matter of expression even more than of feature, and it was in this respect that our friend's countenance was supremely eloquent. (p. 18)

James's "discriminating observer" has his task of interpretation cut out for him, however, since "eloquence" – like any form of visual or verbal rhetoric – is difficult to deal with. One might "perfectly have measured" the American's countenance "and yet have been at a loss to describe it."

> It had that typical vagueness which is not vacuity, that blankness which is not simplicity, that look of being committed to nothing in particular, of standing in an attitude of general hospitality to the chances of life, of being very much at one's own disposal, so characteristic of many American faces. (p. 18)

It was the American's eye that

> chiefly told his story; an eye in which innocence and experience were singularly blended. It was full of contradictory suggestions. . . . you could find in it almost anything you looked for. . . . Decision, salubrity, jocosity, prosperity, seem to hover within his call; he is evidently a practical man, but the idea, in his case, has undefined and mysterious boundaries, which invite the imagination to bestir itself on his behalf. (pp. 18–19)

How characteristic of James's early manner of working with the national type this passage is. He urges upon the observer the need to classify in order to complicate; he delineates clearly defined visual categories in order to insinuate mystery and contradiction; with his checklist of viewable things, he acts as the social realist in order "to invite the imagination to bestir itself," and to bestir itself *on behalf* of the observed object – not for the purpose of despising it. This description is no impersonal, coldly objective itemization of scientifically culled details by which "the American" is calipered into submission to charts and measurements; it is more a riot of impressions and readings that prompt subjective responses to a type aureoled about by "undefined and mysterious boundaries." (That many among James's contemporaries did not catch the warmth of the author's interest will be demonstrated a little further on.)

James's preface to the 1907 New York Edition of *The American*

10

states that he got his "first glimpse" of the "interesting case" of his future hero while seated in a horse car.[13] It is apt that the impulse to study the life of one of his compatriots came to James while he rode in a public conveyance. Had not Walt Whitman perfected the categories of national types displayed in *Leaves of Grass* while riding the Brooklyn ferry? Whitman wished to do more than sit beside his fellow Americans; he tried to enter into their lives or – even more vigorously – to absorb them into his own capacious soul. Henry James was content to observe, however, not to assimilate – as much from literary necessity as from personal fastidiousness.

From his young manhood on, James felt his dissociation from his native land. Many factors contributed: a temperament that drew back more than it reached out; the early experience of years of kiting around Europe in the wake of his parents; and the realization that his family was not part of an American culture that relegated its members to the slots of the businessman, the statesman in the vein of Daniel Webster, and the tipsy man of leisure, while leaving no room for the student (which is how his father was forced to define his vague activities as writer, lecturer, philosopher, and reformer to his inquiring sons).[14] Americans generally took little interest in the artist – the identity James had chosen for himself, which eventually led him to live abroad, away from the nation that seemed to have no name or use for his aspirations.

However dissociated Henry James felt at the start of his elected vocation as "the restless analyst" of "the American Scene" (to allude to the characterizing type he allocated to himself in the book of that title, published in 1905), he actively attempted both to "know" Americans and to place himself somewhere within that special category. How else was he to attain the sense of form he craved above all things in order to further his career as an observer of cultural differences and to stabilize his view of himself as a man of his times?

To ask what Henry James made of the American character in an attempt to meet both professional needs and personal requirements is rather like calling for a resumé of the writings he produced over a fifty-year period between 1865 and 1915. It must suffice here to single out two segments from the American material compiled by a man who felt himself an outsider wherever he happened to be, yet who was avid *to look inside* and who thereby brought the talents (and the limitations) of the spectator to the question formulated as early as 1782 by Hector St. John de Crèvecoeur when that "foreigner" asked, "What is an American?"[15]

In the first instance, James at seventy-one looks back upon several events that transpired in his eighteenth and nineteenth years during the early months of the Civil War; in the second, James in 1878 (the year after the completion of *The American*) responds in print to another American's remarks concerning their countrymen at large in Europe. In both cases (the retrospective view from 1914 of the events of 1861–2 and the on-the-spot testimony of 1878), we catch James seeking out the American type, not to discredit its use as a descriptive instrument but to render it fully and fairly. We witness James attempting *to feel* like an American, or at the very least to understand how we act as national types. In neither case does James wish merely *to see* Americans or to see them as totally "other" than himself.

In the second volume of his memoirs, *Notes of a Son and Brother,* James recalls his arrival in 1862 at Cambridge, Massachusetts. The James family had only recently returned to the United States, and the nineteen-year-old's declared desire was to "rinse my mouth of the European aftertaste in order to do justice to whatever of the native bittersweet might offer itself in congruous vessels."[16] James in 1914 willingly admits of his younger self "that my American consciousness had hitherto been after all and at the best singularly starved" by its long exposure to Europe. He was "after," therefore, "an initiation, at least by the intelligence," of "data in the American kind." He realized that, for all his readiness to study the American character, "far more of the supposed total was I inevitably to miss than to gather to my use. But I might gather what I could, and therein was exactly the adventure."

The greatest obstacle to James's ability to gain "the supposed total" was the fact that, although he was old enough to join with other young male Americans in killing and being killed in the Civil War then underway, he did not embark upon *that* "adventure." Neither he nor his elder brother William served in the forces of the Union Army, even though his younger brothers Wilky and Bob did. Still, Henry James sensed that "The War had by itself of course, on the ground I speak of, communicated something of the quality, or rather of the quantity, otherwise deficient" in the development of his own "starved" sense of himself as an American.

The young James wished to enlarge the scope of his American consciousness, but it was, he realized, "an apprehension without a language or a channel." Such a language and channel might have been his had he gone into battle.[17] As it was, he was restricted to the gawking and gaping from the sidelines that he had nurtured as his private approach to life's "scenes" ever since he had been the Small Boy described in the first volume of his memoirs. "Poor other visitations, comparatively, had had to suffice for me."

Such a visitation came to James on an afternoon in July 1861 that he spent at "a vast gathering of invalid and convalescent troops, under canvas and in roughly improvised shanties" located in Portsmouth Grove on the Rhode Island coast. Walking at random through the camp, the eighteen-year-old James felt that he was at least establishing a relation with "the American soldier in his multitude" – the type in all of its variety. James eagerly responded to this type and drew from his visit an impression of the American male at war as one characterized by "his abandonment to a rueful humour, to a stoic reserve which could yet melt, a relation with him once established, into a rich communicative confidence."

During his absorbed stroll among the wounded at Portsmouth Grove, James attempted to analyze "the aspects strictly native to our social and seasonal air" – complete with "colour and form, accent and quality" – that had "scarce less 'authority'" than those obtained in "the glazed halls of some school of natural history." He realized just the same that his imaginative merger with the American soldier was possible only because "our common Americanism carried with it . . . such a disclosed freshness and strangeness, working, as I might say, over such gulfs of dissociation." Walt Whitman, who had also wandered among the wounded during the war, had the knack of naming Americans because he was one of them; James claimed that he responded just as acutely to his countrymen because they were to some extent "the others."[18]

Throughout James's brief sojourn at the Harvard Law School in

1862, he continued his exercises in the identification of national types by means of experienced dissociation. His fellow students may have concentrated their attention on torts in the classroom, but James was far busier adding "young members of a single type" to his "imagined hall of congruous specimens." As he cast his eyes around the circle of his Harvard classmates, James had two aims, as always: to single out the type and to "string together for exhibition" examples of "differentiation" among the types of the type. His second aim was often thwarted by "the stiff law by which, on the whole American ground, division of *type*, in the light of opposition and contrast, was more and more to break down for me and fail." He concluded, "The difficulty with the type about me was that, in its monotony, beginning and ending with itself, it *had* no connections and suggested none."

There were, however, those rare occasions in Cambridge when James came across "a lone courageous creature" who reached out to "worlds" – to "great far-off reservoirs, of a different mixture altogether, another civility and complexity" than the general blur that defeats the search for distinctiveness of kind. There was his friend G. A. J., who "reached westward, westward even of New York, and southward at least as far as Virginia." In 1862 James, the young lawyer manqué, could hardly know that by cultivating his early habit of seeking out persons who expanded the meaning of "Americanism," he was in training to formulate the literary method by which he brought Christopher Newman into being thirteen years later. He did realize, though, that he was early "opening [himself] to perceptions."

> I was getting furiously American, in the big sense I invoked, through this felt growth of an ability to reach out westward, southward, anywhere, everywhere. . . . thus there dawned upon me the grand possibility that, charm for charm, the American, the assumed, the postulated, would, in the particular case of its really acting, count double; whereas the European paid for being less precarious [in his situation within an established culture] by being also less miraculous.

Over the course of his long life, Henry James never fully came to terms with his conviction that Americans lacked the connections, culture, civility, and complexity that Europeans possessed by virtue of their immersion in history, but while still in his teens, he had begun to suspect that there was "the grand possibility" that the American would "count double" and, further, that the person who aspired to become an artist in a country generally indifferent to his concerns could "become one just by being American enough."

On April 18, 1878, an article entitled "The American Colony in France" appeared in *The Nation* over the initials I.M. The author, one Frederick Sheldon, wrote of that special breed of Americans found in residence abroad or passing through Europe on their restless travels. Throughout his essay Sheldon implies that such Americans were not what he was. His article is deeply critical of what he observes on two fronts: It speaks against the members of the American enclave as viewed by the French and as assessed by Americans like himself who watch his countrymen being watched with contempt by the Parisians. Sheldon also gets his licks in against the wandering American tourist whose "ignorance of custom and etiquette" makes him "utterly unconscious of the disgust he is producing" and against the motley residue of Americans who remain once the tourists depart – people who stay on in Europe for reasons of "Health, education of children, study or science or art."[19] (The type, that is, into which the James family tended to fall during its several sojourns of the 1840s and 1850s.) But Sheldon's main fire is leveled against the "idle, aimless lives" of "the Colonie Americain" that exists "Above and beyond these waifs and strays." Snobs of the first order, these expatriates display in their "uncomfortable self-consciousness a want of confidence in themselves"; this makes them, in turn, quick to look down upon the " 'low' American" who wanders into their midst. Sheldon rather favors this latter type – the same one that Henry James had recently singled out as "the American" in his novel of the preceding year. This type "may have little taste or appreciation of art," Sheldon acknowledges, "but he really believes in himself and in his country."

Six months after Sheldon's essay appeared in *The Nation* James's response was published in the same magazine on October 3, 1878. In his piece, James speaks of the many examples he has observed of "the national character" that have had "free play in European hotels and railroad stations."[20] He notes, too, the "specimens of the unattached young American lady" that engage the attention of her compatriots in residence abroad "who are always ready to be a party to national self-analysis."[21] This said, James moves swiftly to take a different approach than Sheldon to the problem of evaluating national types. He wishes to introduce "some new ideas" of the kind that ought to have occurred, but unfortunately have not, to other observers of the American type.

"Americans in Europe are *outsiders*," James states; this is "the great point." James's second "great point" is that he wants to drop the use of distancing terms that fix Americans as foreign objects eyed by one who is himself an "outsider" to their condition. James takes up the pronoun "we," thereby making all citizens of the United States secret sharers of that special condition experienced by the American set at odds with the rest of the Western world:

> As a people we are out of European society; the fact seems to us incontestable, be it regrettable or not. We are not only out of the European circle politically and geographically; we are out of it socially, and for excellent reasons. We are the only great people of the civilized world that is a pure democracy, and we are the only great people that is exclusively commercial. Add the remoteness represented by these facts to our great and painful geographical remoteness, and it will be easy to see why to be known in Europe as an American is to enjoy an imperfect reciprocity. (p. 208)

"Aliens," "absentee," "forsaken": these are other words by which James defines the way Americans abroad are viewed by those entrenched in their native culture. It is a pity that such words make "the European take the American, as an American, by so much the less *au serieux*," but James, on his part, is determined to take the American seriously. How not, since *being American* is the part he too plays before the world? Frederick Sheldon's self-distancing approach to the subject has the tendency to covert him into a snob without a country who does to the American colony in Paris what members of that colony do to the rest of their compatriots – dismiss them with the phrase "you Americans." In contrast, James places himself *within* the category "American." By now he realizes that his commitment to study what it means to be

16

like that type requires that he take the rough with the smooth. Absent from the 1878 essay is the priggish snobbery that James, at twenty-six, expressed in a letter home while traveling through Europe in 1869:

> There is but one word to use in regard to [Americans] – vulgar, vulgar, vulgar. Their ignorance – their stingy, defiant, grudging attitude towards everything European – their perpetual reference of all things to some American standard or precedent which exists only in their own unscrupulous wind-bags – and then our unhappy poverty of voice, of speech and of physiognomy – these things glare at you hideously.[22]

Even in the midst of this diatribe of 1869, James had to insert an important and flattering qualification, doing it significantly through the use of the associative "we": "On the other hand, we seem a people of *character,* seem to have energy, capacity, and intellectual stuff in ample measure." Three days later, he appended a further proviso to the bottom of his letter, whether to placate his parents or himself: "I *have* seen some nice Americans and I still love my country."

The sticking point for James in 1869, as it would continue to be throughout his life, was the issue of culture. As he noted in the essay of 1878, the American is "the modern man"; he is not the man of the past who possesses history – that is, the manners and memories out of which culture is made. Precisely defined, the American is "the modern man with *culture* quite left out." In his response to Sheldon's article and in the wake of his own full-length appraisal of Christopher Newman, James finds more to say than his shallow assessment of the type in the letter of 1869 allowed. Now he acknowledges that the type contains both "argumentative national self-consciousness" and "a profound, imperturbable unsuspectingness" – a quality that "has always been, we suggest, the mark of great nationalities."

Of course, when James says, "The great innocence of the usual American tourist is perhaps his most general quality," he does not really believe he is describing himself; yet James is ready to defend the deplorable trait of "innocence" against the way "it is harshly interpreted" by those "sophisticated Europeans" who "set it down once for all as very vulgar." James is clearly at one with "the sophisticated spectator" who, when eying his visiting countrymen, cannot ignore the poor impressions such Americans make on the ear and the eye; he admits that this type is "ill-made, ill-mannered, ill-dressed," and asks almost querulously, "*Are* we the worst-looking people in the world?" Still, James has other observations to make, of a density missing from Sheldon's essentially superficial glance.

Although James never gives approval to ignorance masked as innocence, he senses that ignorance as the primary defining term for the American is itself somewhat of a red herring. At those moments when ignorance of self and of the ways of the rest of the world *does* function as a clue to the national character, that ignorance reveals its capacity to fluctuate. A believer in history defined as a matter of developing phases, James puts forward the notion that Americans were once more "conscious" than they now are in the 1870s. Today, "by a sort of Hegelian unfolding, this type is on its way to become unconscious again." More changes are on the way. Impelled by still another shift, "the American in Europe often enters into what we have called the conscious phase by a great deal of irritation." Caustic Europeans, it turns out, serve the Hegelian process by jolting Americans back into a fuller awareness of their own nature. The path to self-knowledge is hardly smooth. As James emphasizes, there are "many anomalies and crookedness in the lot of the conscious American" caught in the hard stare of "the others."

James mounts an arresting defense of the often maligned type of the American in the final paragraph of his essay of 1878. He appears to be rediscovering what he had begun to accept as his personal birthright during the years of the Civil War. What the conscious American is learning, James concludes, is how ignorant Europeans are of *his* country: "it is hardly too much to say that as a general thing, as regards this subject, the European mind is a perfect blank." Americans may be regrettably lacking in knowledge of Europe, but in its place "they have a certain amount of imagination." "In respect to the United States the European imagination is motionless." It commits "something ridiculous" when it "leaves out a country as large as an aggregation of European kingdoms." James brings his appraisal to its close with a statement that has the effect of a flung gauntlet:

> It is comparatively easy to confess yourself a provincial if you really come from a province; but if you have been brought up among "big things" of every kind the admission requires an effort. On the whole, the American in Europe may be spoken of as a provincial who is terribly bent upon taking, in the fulness of ages, his revenge. (p. 209)

Of all men, James has come down on the side of an American self-esteem grounded in the sense of the nation's bigness! Great of geography *and* of spirit; great of *possession*. Just as he had in his letter home of 1869, he speaks as an advocate for "a people of *character*" – a special breed with whom he wishes to ally himself, since "we" can claim "energy, capacity and intellectual stuff in ample measure." James never got over the fact that, by the accident of the Old World's extended past, the French "had" culture by whose means they as a people commanded richness of social reference. Having culture did not mean that Frenchmen as individuals were big or profound by nature. Quite the opposite. As Henry James wrote to his brother William on July 4, 1876, he was convinced of "their bottomless superficiality."[23] Whenever the American had to contend with the static imagination and empty superficiality of the European, he could aspire to take, "in the fulness of ages, his revenge." Henry James – more conscious than most and possessed of an imagination that was anything but motionless – did not have to wait that long. By 1876 he had found out enough about the various forms of Americanism in history to feel the inspiration to provide that national type with its necessary literary form.

3

Defining the American character was a national pastime in the nineteenth century among those who claimed the racial right to separate ethnic sheep from goats, usually on the basis of their own long-term settlement in the New World and their alleged possession of "correct" connections with acceptable Northern European

19

antecedents. Categorizations of this sort stemmed, of course, from a series of misperceptions, the most obvious of which was the notion that there is such an entity as *the* American. This is not to say that the ablest of the classifiers paid no attention to diversity and complexity within the type they had elected to stand as the nation's primary representative. The American type contained the subtypes of male and female; young and old; westerner, easterner, and southerner; wealthy and poor; banker and farmer. Certainly, individual examples of the type were depicted by its portraitists with the "undefined and mysterious boundaries" of the kind Henry James pointed to in his initial description of Christopher Newman. The hard-core nativists continued, however, to insist upon the reality of a homogeneity derived from the particular attributes expected of the American character: Northern European caucasian by race, tradition, and derivation (English, Scottish, Welsh, German, Dutch, Swedish, perhaps French); Protestant by religion; English-speaking by birth or through rapid assimilation of the prescribed mother tongue. Had not Crèvecoeur replied to the question he asked in 1782, "What is an American?" with a statement of his faith in the melting pot principle applied to a new country whose ingredients are related in kind even before they fall into place within the grand whole of the New World experience?[24]

From the outset in the colonies, and later in the newly formed republic, the naked eye and acute ear had had to take note of *all the others* who made up the American populace: native Americans, blacks imported as slaves directly from Africa or by way of the Caribbean, Jews, Italians, Irish Catholics, Slavs. Once the habit of mental cataloging got underway, the type of "the true American" was set against whatever other racial and national types existed in the United States who were not considered American.

Even Walt Whitman's celebration of diversity of races and tongues in *Leaves of Grass* was predicated upon his belief that there was a discernible and essential unity within the rampant multiplicity; but most nineteenth-century definitions of the American character during the same decades when the society was undergoing increasing rents and divisions did not bother with Whitmanian visions of a Kosmos capable of encompassing union. When Mark Twain added his note to *Adventures of Huckleberry Finn,* in explanation of the various dialects in his tale[25] – "the Missouri negro dialect; the extremist form of the backwoods Southwestern dialect; the ordinary 'Pike County' dialect; and four modified varieties of this last" – he was defining the gradations of sounds and diction within basic American speech patterns. Yiddish, Cantonese, Gaelic, Calabrian, Sioux, or Greek dialects were not his concern, nor of anyone else out to delineate the American.

It *is* possible to detect subtle degrees in the assumptions and motives that lay behind the craving for the phantom homogeneity that dominated the minds of many during the later decades of the nineteenth century. Some asserted the wholeness of the general social fabric in the face of disruptive factors that they realized gave the lie to all notions of cultural harmony. Others managed to shut out the realization that the accepted national image of the Yankee was myth, not reality; they did this by rigorously separating "we" from "they." A few argued that anyone of any kind and degree who lived within the political system of the United States ought to be called an American by right – and accident – of place, but most drew back from giving up the comfort they derived from living by categories that flattered their sense of racial self-esteem. This provided cold comfort for the nativists, of course, when with the passage of time the increase in the number of insistent "others" – the alien faces, voices, and customs – brought into harsh focus what had been true all along: that there is no such social animal as the American.

In the years just prior to World War I, Henry James looked back to his youth during the period of the Civil War as a time when he (even he) had believed he could sense what Americanism was, but he remembered that belief in order to record its naiveté. In the passage from *Notes of a Son and Brother* previously cited (where James describes the Rhode Island army camp as "the glazed halls of some school of natural history" that taught the eighteen-year-old "the aspects strictly native to our social and seasonal air"), he inserts the observations of the man of seventy-one.[26] The older James compares the ease and pleasure with which the young James had enjoyed his discovery of the American type with "the restrictions imposed on directness of sympathy by the awful admixtures of to-day." After 1900, whenever men like James returned from Europe to visit the United States, they departed from a continent where, supposedly, "homogeneity and its entailed fraternity, its easy contacts, still may seem to work"; they encountered the new masses who afforded "this shock – the recognition, by any sensibility at all reflective, of the point where our national theory of absorption, assimilation and conversion appallingly breaks down."

The James of 1914 realizes that the differences he finds in comparing the United States of the 1860s and the nation after 1900 are as much the result of a shift in his awareness – between what he then perceived and now perceives – as they are changes in the new demographics. By 1914 James's emphasis is upon the "unconsciousness" felt by the boy in 1861 "of any difficulty for knowing in the old, the comparatively brothering, conditions what an American at least *was.*" When Henry James wrote *The American* fifteen years after his visit to the army camps of the 1860s, he was still holding to the faith that he, together with the rest of his countrymen, had no problem – existing as they did within "the old, the comparatively brothering, conditions" – in knowing the nature of the American.

4

The Philadelphia Centennial Exposition of 1876 and the dedication of the Statue of Liberty in New York's harbor in 1886 provided the nation with the official icons that encouraged the huddled masses of "the others" to become Americans by means of "absorption, assimilation and conversion." James's *The American* aligns perfectly with the perceptions and misconceptions shaping the imagination of many of the country's citizens during those decades. It is little wonder, then, that the reception given at the time to James's novel by the critics and reviewers focuses upon three interrelated questions: how well James captured the American type through his fictional portrayal of Christopher Newman, whether the narrative is realistic or romantic in the methods it uses to render this type accurately, and if the story comes to an ending appropriate to the character of such an American.

The American received a fair amount of attention in the magazine world of both England and the United States. Thirteen American notices appeared, including reviews in major publications such as *The Nation* and the *Atlantic Monthly, The Galaxy, Scribner's Magazine, Appleton's Journal,* and *The North American Review.* Eight reviews came out in the British journals, *The Athenaeum, The Spectator,* and *The British Quarterly Review* among them.[27] American reviewers naturally had more at stake in the matter of James's skill at portraying the American than did the British critics; it was ostensibly one of their own they had to size up. The reviews divided rather neatly between the ones that liked Newman and those that bristled at the notion that their nation should be represented by *that* particular kind of American.

The reviewer for *The Nation* in the issue of January 11, 1877, praised James's story even before the *Atlantic Monthly* serialization reached its conclusion:

> We confess to having had at first a feeling of irritation at being called upon to take an interest in a specimen of a type which, as a type, is, to say the least, not aesthetically attractive. The self-made American, who has suddenly grown rich by "operations" of one kind or another, and has taken himself and his wealth to Europe, is a familiar enough character in literature, but usually the character has been made a comic one, and we have been called upon to laugh at the ridiculous figure cut by our compatriot in the gilded saloons of the effete but critical Europeans, or at his shocking display of ignorance and barbarism as he wanders through "specimen ruins" and "specimen galleries." Mr. James, however, has placed before himself a very different task. He has undertaken to make use of this same type as a serious character in a love story.

According to *The Nation,* James's placement of Newman in the midst of the Parisian "atmosphere of perfectly cold politeness and perfect inanity" has the fortunate consequence of setting off "our American barbarian lover" to advantage. That Newman is able "to interest the reader" is "striking proof of Mr. James's power as a novelist." Though the reviewer felt that "it would be rash to express an opinion [on the story] till it is completed," he believed it was "safe to say that it is by far the most important contribution to American fiction made for a long time."

The Galaxy of July 1877 was not as pleased with James's novel, "which is so good that we regret very much that it is not better." Among the reasons given for its comparative failure, the reviewer singled out "the title of his book and the inferences which it measurably warrants abroad."

> Mr. Christopher Newman is certainly a fair representative of a certain sort, and a very respectable sort, of American; but he is not such a man that Mr. James, himself an American living in Europe, is warranted in setting him up before the world as "*The* American." Men like Newman are already too commonly regarded as the best product, if not the only product, of two hundred and fifty years of American life, and a hundred of republican institutions. But let us argue a little *ad hominem,* and ask Mr. James if Christopher Newman represents the larger number of his associates when he is at home. We fancy not. Why then put him forth thus set up on the pedestal of the definite article? If Mr. James had chosen to write his novel with Newman for hero, and to call it by his name . . . and to let Newman go as a representative of a certain kind of American who gets rich in California, very well; but to have an American hold this man up to the world as *the* American is not highly satisfactory.

At this juncture, *The Galaxy* review heats up to its argument:

> Whereas, Newman, although an honorable and respectable man, intelligent in his way, and well-behaved enough, is so entirely lacking in attractive personal qualities, and although not exactly uncouth, so raw in his manner, that no one wonders why the Bellegardes, being at heart dishonorable people, seize the first opportunity of getting rid of him. He is after all only just what Mr. James makes them call him, "a commercial person," which he might be, and yet be all the rest that he is not. Our only wonder is how a woman like Mme. de Cintré can be brought to look upon him with eyes of personal favor.

The *Scribner's* review of the same month took exactly the opposite view. It decided that Newman was so much "the best typical American sort as to afford a safe basis for the highest hopes that might be built upon it." Indeed, James's portrait was of a man "Big, rich, frank, simple-hearted, straightforward, and triumphantly successful" – one who "satisfied us entirely by his genuine and hearty manliness." Unfortunately, the reviewer felt that James failed to sustain the interest he had created in his hero at the start. By the story's conclusion, "we are made angry by his own failure to comprehend the character he had created." That is, James had failed as a writer by allowing Newman to do something so un-American as to fail in his endeavors.

Appleton's Journal of August 1877 liked *The American*. The reviewer found "deep and many-sided interest" in a narrative in which "the individual is subordinated to the social type, and beneath and around the persons whose little drama nominally occupies the stage we are made to see and feel the warring of two opposing civilizations." In marked contrast to these words of approval, *The Catholic World* in December of the following year judged that James's book was "not interesting." Foreigners, "reading it as a representative American novel, would be sorely puzzled to know if Newman, whom Mr. James characterizes as not only 'a fine American' but also 'a fine man,' is a good specimen of our national manhood." Noting with contempt that Newman's "figures of speech are drawn from the prize-ring and equally refined associations," the reviewer testily finds "nothing in *The American* to improve anybody's morals or manners" since "there is not a gentleman or a lady between its covers." The reviewer concludes by questioning

> whether the bad types of our men and women are not caricatured enough by foreigners; whether it is commendable in American authors not merely to lampoon the national foibles which ought to be lampooned but to paint an illiterate and audacious gawk in a pretendedly fine frame and label him a representative American?

How safe from the threat of national self-criticism the reviewer for the London *Athenaeum* must have felt when he commented upon *The American* in July 1877! "Mr. James's 'American' will interest English readers greatly, as a clever presentment of a characteristic type of his countrymen, in search of adventures in the paradise [Paris] to which good Americans go." The English reviewer for *The Academy* of July 14, 1877, was also released from anxiety over the misdemeanors of his own national type, but he was unhappy with the novel all the same; he missed the expected pleasure to be had from reading about another country's typical citizens. He complained on behalf of his readers that

we wish we could like [James's] chief figures. The portrait of his
countryman must of course be taken as accurate, and is evidently
sympathetic. But if not only the *naif* consciousness and avowal of
being as good as anybody else, but also the inability to understand
how the anybody else may possibly differ from him on this point, be
taken from life, the defect of repulsion strikes us as a serious one.

The issue of the ability of readers to accept James's portrait of
Christopher Newman as the American, and/or to find comfort in
their perception of that type as likeable, has not faded with the
passage of time. One hundred years later, critics are still judging
the merits of James's novel in light of how well they consider that
James captured the national type and to what purposes. From the
beginning, James knew he had to contend with reviewers and
critics, good and bad, as suggested by his comment to his brother
William in a letter of June 28, 1877, that *The American* was to be
surveyed for the *Saturday Review* of London, "probably indif-
ferently well, as 'tis by Walter Pollock, a very amiable mediocrity."[28] He could hardly be surprised at the critics' continuing
disagreements concerning the accuracy of his responses to the
American type.[29]

Leon Edel believes that James wrote into Newman's character
all that he himself disliked about his homeland. Kermit Vanderbilt
finds Newman grievously flawed and no hero, whereas Edward R.
Zietlow concentrates upon Newman's highly questionable "legal
and moral" hubris, which leads him to destroy evidence concerning Mme. de Bellegarde's crime against her husband. On the other
hand, R. W. Butterfield's essay emphasizes the remark James
made in a letter to Howells of March 30, 1877: "I have written my
story from Newman's side of the wall."[30] Oscar Cargill also believes that James affirmed Newman's cause and concludes that
James "wrote as an emotionally aroused American." Though Butterfield agrees that James remained on Newman's side in his sympathies, he argues that James located the emotional pivot of the
narrative "in mid Atlantic, now leaning West, now tilting back
East." It is James's ambivalence, which places him in no fixed
relation to the complex issues raised by any assessment of New
World culture pitted against Old World societies, that highlights

Cleanth Brooks's essay, Mutlu Blasing's "Double Focus in *The American*," and James W. Tuttleton's chapter, "Henry James: The Superstitious Valuation of Europe" (see the Bibliography).

If recent critical examinations of the "complex fate" of being American (to draw upon James's own phrase) reiterate the original question, "What is an American?" and if they continue to emphasize the dualities contained within the type recognized by the shrewdest of the early reviewers, new concerns have been added. In the 1950s and 1960s, "innocence" became a major critical litmus test applied to literary treatments of the national experience. Under this new emphasis, the word itself has shifted from a reference to purity to one of knowing; from childlike freshness and charming naiveté to the dangers faced by Americans lacking sufficient awareness. Critics from England, Japan, and India — countries long on experience — find *The American* a particularly fascinating text for measuring the strengths and weaknesses of a nation that once took the type of the American Adam (portrayed as Newman, Huck Finn, Jay Gatsby, or Thomas Sutpen) to its collective bosom.[31]

Another topic of interest has been incorporated into the critical agenda that directly influences the approach taken to interpretations of James's novel; it is one that has helped to undercut the potential speciousness of the notion of Newman as the wide-eyed innocent. Constance Rourke's appraisal of *The American* in her 1931 study, *American Humor*, pointed to a significant aspect of Newman's Americanism — the "comical" nature of his "Yankee" response to experience. In 1961 Frederick J. Hoffman also remarked upon James's use of humor vis-à-vis his rendition of the national identity in an essay aptly subtitled "Henry James and the American Self," while Richard Poirier devoted a chapter to the subject in his *The Comic Sense of Henry James* and William T. Stafford stressed the necessity to judge James's literary success in just those terms in "The Ending of Henry James's *The American*." The point to keep in mind is that when critics focus in upon Newman's sense of humor, effectively rendered by his creator through the techniques of literary comedy, they are continuing to discuss a central aspect of American character itself. As Henry

James had observed in 1879, humor is the American's particular "secret" − his special, essential value, that element that takes the place of what Europeans experience as "culture."[32]

5

Both early and later, reviewers and critics eyed the formalistic manner in which Henry James presented his portrait of Christopher Newman. Whether they were fully aware of the fact or not, their observations also formed part of the pursuit of the underlying thematic question, what is an American? To discuss the artistry of James's narrative stance, or the genre form he chose to carry his plot, or the nature of the story's conclusion is not merely to discuss the merits of those several literary solutions taken by a youthful author still in the process of discovering effective forms for his art; it is to discuss the forms Americanism itself was taking in James's imagination.

On May 17, 1877, *The Independent* chided James for his "polished, philosophical, and absolutely cold-blooded story." James was reproached for being a "fastidious writer" capable only of "supercilious culture and haughty accuracy."[33] The reviewer for *The Literary World* of July 1877 acknowledged "the brilliancy of [the] literary execution" of *The American,* but (like the reviewer for *The Independent*) he deplored its lack of soul, sympathy, and seriousness. James's characters were presented for "inspection," not for the readers' moral edification or emotional satisfaction. James's chilly style − derived from his analytic qualities and "the undertone of sarcasm that betrays the *critic*" − was also cited by *The Literary Table* of August 30 of the same year. Even the generally approving review from *The North American Review* of September had reservations about the cost to the novel's appeal resulting from the author's concentration upon technical skills and the "intellectual side" that forced readers to believe they were "attending merely on a series of experiments − a kind of psychological clinic."

Critical remarks of this nature are intimately related to the question of whether James *liked* what he dissected with the seeming skill and cold accuracy of the scientist. It was generally assumed by the early reviewers that warm fellow feeling and sincere national

28

pride were the proper attitudes for authors to take when rendering portraits of their compatriots. Not finding these qualities in James's writing in regard either to his fictional characters in general or to his representation of the American way of life, reviewers concluded that James was a cold fish and a lackluster supporter of his homeland. They were not aware of the argument James had mounted as early as 1865 in his own role as a reviewer of Walt Whitman's collection of Civil War poems, "Drum Taps." James's anonymous piece for *The Nation* called attention to the difference he found between great themes and pretentious rhetoric; it pointed up his belief in the need for the writer's removal from the immediate site of emotion-filled events:[34]

> *Of course* the tumult of a battle is grand, the results of a battle tragic, and the untimely deaths of young men a theme for elegies. But he is not a poet who merely reiterates these plain facts *ore rotundo.* He only sings them worthily who views them from a height.

James in 1865 objected to "minds which are bullied by the *accidents* of the affair" and which foolishly attempt to incarnate ideas rather than to reveal them. He spoke out with a twenty-two-year-old's fervor about the necessity of concealing patriotic feelings within an appropriate literary form, one possessed of the state of self-possession:

> To be positive one must have something to say; to be positive requires reason, labor, and art; and art requires, above all things, a suppression of one's self, a subordination of one's self to an idea. . . . To become adopted as a national poet, it is not enough to discard everything in particular and to accept everything in general, to amass crudity upon crudity, to discharge the undigested contents of your blotting-book into the lap of the public. . . . Your personal qualities — the vigor of your temperament, the manly independence of your nature, the tenderness of your heart — these facts are impertinent. You must be *possessed,* and you must strive to possess your possession. If in your striving you break into divine eloquence, then you are a poet. If the idea which possesses you is the idea of your country's greatness, then you are a national poet; and not otherwise.

James's precocious realization in 1865 that a national spokesman ought to assume the authorial stance of one who observes, inspects, and analyzes "from a height" in order better to comprehend and declare the American character was matched by his own efforts throughout the 1870s to select the literary genre best suited to his self-appointed task. Whether the national type is most effectively defined by means of realism or romance has become one of the leading questions taken up by recent critics of *The American*. Contemporary reviewers have lingered most frequently upon the surface of James's writing, but what seizes our attention these days is the book's narrative structure – as one that follows the mandates of the realistic novel or takes up the romance form of the melodrama.

There is good reason for this shift in critical focus. James himself insisted on the importance of the issue of genre in the preface he wrote for the 1907 edition of *The American*. In looking back over the thirty years that separated the novel's first appearance from its current revival in the New York Edition, James stated that he only now recognized the appeal Newman's story had originally had for him as a baffled figure caught up in a romance melodrama of evil versus good: "I value in my retrospect nothing so much as the lively light on the romantic property of my subject that I had not expected to encounter."[35] The ruminating author of 1907 also testified to the way "the romantic property" is entangled inexplicably with those elements commonly called "realistic."

> If in "The American" I invoked the romantic association without malice prepense, yet with a production of the romantic effect that is for myself unmistakeable, the occasion is of the best perhaps for penetrating a little the obscurity of that principle. By what art or mystery, what craft of selection, omission or commission, does a given picture of life appear to us to surround its theme, its figures and images, with the air of romance while another picture close beside it may affect us as steeping the whole matter in the element of reality?

This said, James's preface proceeds to lay out the by-now famous twin definitions of the romantic and the real:

> The real represents to my perception the things we cannot possibly *not* know, sooner or later, in one way or another; it being but one of the accidents of our hampered state, and one of the incidents of their quantity and number, that particular instances have not yet come our way. The romantic stands, on the other hand, for the things that, with all the facilities in the world, all the wealth and all

the courage and all the wit and all the adventure, we never *can* directly know; the things that can reach us only through the beautiful circuit and subterfuge of our thought and our desire.

In his essay for this collection, Peter Brooks directly addresses James's evolving relationship to the complex forms of romance/melodrama and realistic fiction; he establishes that James's early experiments in literary forms that culminated in *The American* in 1877 act as a crucial turning point in James's artistic career. Brooks quite rightly points to the French influences upon James's choice of genre that led the somewhat apprehensive William James to beg his brother not to indulge in "too many traces of Gallicism in manner."[36] (William's admonitions were quite different from the aspersions cast by *The Literary World* of July 1877 upon the supposed amorality of *The American*, which "comes perilously near being a French novel, from which may the good Lord deliver us!") Mark Seltzer's essay approaches the realism/romance debate from the direction of economic theory and aligns the movement of the narrative with the ruling passion of "physical capital." I, in turn, wish to emphasize that James's struggle to locate his imagination at the point between "the things we cannot possibly *not* know, sooner or later, in one way or another" and "the things that, with all the facilities in the world, all the wealth and all the courage and all the wit and all the adventure, we never *can* directly know" was yet another aspect of his lifelong effort to know the American and the nature of Americanism. What James refers to here is not only a description of the real and the romantic; it also expresses Newman's confident belief that nothing can bar him as an American from what he needs to understand; it expresses just as powerfully the world of mysteries that prevents Americans of Newman's stamp from appropriating all knowledge and all power.

The third area of concern that thrusts itself insistently upon careful readers of *The American* is the ending James gave to his narrative; rather, to his *several* endings, since he eventually complicated the consideration we give to any narrative conclusion by writing closings other than the one that finished the *Atlantic Monthly* serial and the early book editions. Long before James patched together a conventionally happy fourth-act curtain for the stage version of the story in 1892, and before he revised the language and inferences of the final paragraphs that appeared in the 1907 New York Edition, his first audiences made known their displeasure over the original ending of Newman's adventures.

The unfavorable reactions came down to the readers' desire for a conclusion with everyone alive and well and the lovers united in permanent married bliss. The cleverest reviewers acknowledged that mere wish fulfillment does not furnish a sound basis for literary success; they advanced as the reasonable cause for their dissatisfaction the fact that a sad ending was inconsistent with Newman's supposed character as a strong-willed man capable of getting whatever he goes after. From their perspective, Americans like Newman do not fail, and American lovers consistently triumph through passionate action. The critics for *The Nation,* the *Atlantic Monthly, Scribner's,* and *Appleton's Journal* decided, therefore, that the characteristic American passion and force were lacking; no wonder they believed that James's unhappy ending betrayed the promises given in the first half of the narrative. James had undercut the strengths commonly attributed at that time to the American because he had substituted a faulty notion of national character for the real thing. As the reviewer for *The Eclectic* of August 1877 put it,

> the reader is dissatisfied with the manner in which "The American" ends, not because it is painful, but because it mars the conception which he has been led to form of the two principal characters in the story; because it seems incongruous with what has gone before; and because it is manifestly the result, not of spontaneously-acting natural causes, but of a preexistent social theory in the author's mind.[37]

The issues raised by *The Eclectic* and the other reviews of 1877 live on in the minds of more recent critics, but readers since 1907 face an even trickier task in sorting out responses to the question of whether James's novel ends well as a literary structure consistent both with its internal patterns and as a portrayal of American character. Their interpretations are complicated by the shifts in tone, wording, and nuance that James introduced in the revisions he made for the 1907 edition.[38]

The plot of *The American* does not change as such from 1877 to 1907. Claire de Cintré is still behind convent walls; her brother

Valentin is dead; Newman has lost the woman he wished to marry. But the manner in which the novel's final scene is presented has been unquestionably altered. In the closing lines of the original version, we see Mrs. Tristram confronting Newman, who has tossed the paper containing incriminating evidence against his foes, the Bellegardes, into the flames.

> "It is most provoking," said Mrs. Tristram, "to hear you talk of the 'charge' when the charge is burnt up. Is it quite consumed?" she asked, glancing at the fire.
> Newman assured her that there was nothing left of it.
> "Well then," she said, "I suppose there is no harm in saying that you probably did not make them so very uncomfortable. My impression would be that since, as you say, they defied you, it was because they believed that, after all, you would never really come to the point. Their confidence, after counsel taken of each other, was not in their innocence, nor in their talent for bluffing things off; it was in your remarkable good nature! You see they were right."
> Newman instinctively turned to see if the little paper was in fact consumed; but there was nothing left of it. (p. 309)

When we consult the 1907 version and pick up at the same point in the final scene, we notice that Newman's instinctive reaction to the destroyed piece of evidence is omitted altogether; attention focuses entirely on the pity of Claire's having given up the chance of finding happiness in the arms of a splendid man.

> "It's most provoking," she returned, "to hear you talk of the 'charge' when the charge is burned up. Is it quite consumed?" she asked, glancing at the fire. He assured her there was nothing left of it, and at this, dropping her embroidery, she got up and came near him. "I needn't tell you at this hour how I've felt for you. But I liked you as you are," she said.
> "As I am —?"
> "As you are." She stood before him and put out her hand as for his own, which he a little blankly let her take. "Just exactly as you are," she repeated and very tenderly and beautifully kissed it. Then, "Ah, poor Claire!" she signed as she went back to her place. It drew from him, while his flushed face followed her, a strange inarticulate sound, and this made her but say again: "Yes, a thousand times — poor, poor Claire!"

Royal Gettmann's essay of 1945 provided a detailed analysis of the many alterations James made between his 1877 and 1907 editions, but earlier commentators had already pointed out some of the differences involved and had either supported or attacked James's manipulations of the novel's final scene.[39] During the 1920s alone, J. Robert Herrick opposed, while Theodora Bosanquet and Pelham Edgar spoke in favor of the new Newman.[40] More recently, Roy Harvey Pearce and William Stafford are among those who have stated their preference for the earlier version, whereas Gettmann and Floyd Watkins have argued the merits of the later version.[41] As on the occasions of the heightened umbrage over James's authorial stance (sized up as cool, analytic) and over his treatment of the romance/realism debate (deemed a bit of a muddle), the question of endings once again returns us to the central issue of the national type James continued to turn over in his imagination between 1877 and 1907.[42] Who is the American, the man of unadulterated good nature and innate nobility of action (as the 1907 conclusion might appear to emphasize through its deletion of any sudden recoil on Newman's part when faced with the fact that he has foolishly discarded his best means for revenge) or the man who has perhaps done "the decent thing" by foregoing vindictiveness but who still experiences an instinctual reversion to that "baser" motive (as the 1877 version largely suggests)? Is the American the man of relaxed humor and steady self-confidence or the man who reveals, however briefly, regret over the naiveté that made him falsely value a sense of himself as a good fellow instead of savoring the bitter satisfaction that comes from wielding ruthless power over others?

In 1969 Alina Szala wrote a short note for the journal *Kwartalnik Neofilologiczny* concerning the pirated Polish edition of *The American* published in 1879.[43] The gist of Szala's report is that the Polish translator (who worked directly from a German translation published in Stuttgart in 1878) simplified James's original text past recognition in order "to adapt the protagonist to the popular European notion about Americans." In both the German and the Polish versions, all ends happily with Newman's marriage and his departure with Claire for the United States.

> . . . for a serious artist like James, the national label was only a starting point and a source of dramatic conflict in the novel; as the plot develops, Newman becomes aware of evil and loses his inno-

cent optimism. But that was an artistic subtlety in the concept of human character which exceeded the categories of national stereotypes and was therefore conveniently eliminated from the simplified Polish version, although much of it was retained in the more conscientious Stuttgart translation. What was left in the Polish text was cut strictly to conform to the popular notions: the American remained throughout bold and self-assured, and thus the happy solution of his love troubles came more naturally than in the German version. It is something else that he became scarcely recognizable as a Jamesian character. The Newman portrayed in the Polish text emerges as a stereotype American that flourished on the pages of journalistic accounts of travels in the United States. (p. 64)

Polish readers apparently expected Americans like Newman to succeed without stumbling. A path cleared of all impediments to romance was also demanded by the theater-going public in England as well, and this time Henry James was persuaded to comply with their wants. Leon Edel has marshaled an account of the events that led the English theater manager Edward Compton to talk James into rewriting the ending of the staged version of *The American*.[44] When we read the final lines of the 1892 playscript, we get a glimpse of what audiences clamor to get for the sake of their amusement, whatever the hero's nationality; we see what James was finally willing to do to gain their approval.

> CLAIRE *goes on speaking out loud and clear* [to her brother the Marquis]: "You can carry our mother as well some remarkable news that I've determined — and (looking about to the others) I'm glad you should all *hear* it! — to become Mr. Newman's *wife!*"
> NEWMAN (*springing to her, and as he folds her in his arms*): "That's *just* what I wanted to *see!*"

During the months when James was in Paris completing the final episodes of his story for the *Atlantic Monthly,* he expressed the courage of his convictions to William Dean Howells: "Mme. de Cintré doesn't marry Newman, and I couldn't possibly, possibly, have made her do it. The whole point of the *denouement* was, in the conception of the tale, in his losing her."[45] In March 1877, now in London, James explained at even greater length to Howells that "the interest of the subject was, for me (without my being at all a pessimist) its exemplification of one of those insuperable difficulties which present themselves in people's lives and from which the only issue is by forfeiture – by losing something." In the spring of 1877, James the expatriated American realized that Americans, despite their vaunted national specialness and apparent imperviousness to the fate expected of other mortals, are still vulnerable to the pain exacted by the human condition. Germans, Poles, or the English might believe in the fable of the unique powers of Americans – a fable that would inspire sufficient numbers of them over the ensuing decades to immigrate to the New World so that they might also share in the American dream that promised that one gets whatever one wants, but Henry James knew differently. In both 1877 and 1907, he also knew enough about his native land to portray one of its representatives as an interesting amalgam of opposed reactions to difficult tests, as a man capable of good will and of giving in to the temptation to make revengeful use of power. James did not, however, understand the type well enough to provide full consistency to his tale or his characterizations. The ambiguities of a character of sufficient narrative strength to be both pleasing and unpleasant were not entirely within his authorial control. As a result, definite obstructions to a ready interpretation of the significance of Christopher Newman's actions create ridges along the polished surface of the narrative form, whether in 1877, 1907, or 1987. Although the consequences of James's personal and professional uncertainties guarantee that we today cannot see exactly what the American signified to James as a fictional character and as a possible alter ego, we are able to catch sight of James working out the forms for his own life as an American writer, for the complex views he held about Americans undergoing the processes of self-definition and self-determination, and for the literary techniques (narrative structure, genre, style, authorial stance) he brought to his analysis of that ever provocative, provoking type – *the American*.

The essays in this collection focus on the central figure of the American, analyzing the meaning of Christopher Newman and the novel he inhabits from a series of separate, though related, perspectives. Peter Brooks aligns the principles of the craft of fiction James was in the process of defining during the late 1870s with the complex responses marking James's wary encounters with the inner circle of the French Naturalists; by tracing the route followed by *The American* as it swerved along the beckoning literary paths of the romance and the novel, Brooks's essay points out just where James took an important turn in the development of his narrative forms. John Carlos Rowe examines the political divisions within old and new French society, providing the kind of information it would have been advantageous for Newman to have possessed; he indicates the consequences to Newman's "education" as an innocent abroad of the power plays that take place between the American democrat and Parisian aristocracy. Mark Seltzer and Carolyn Porter each make capital of Newman's position as a prime representative of the American money system. Seltzer focuses upon the double significance of a narrative that is both *about* the consumption of salable commodities and a *reflection* of a capitalistic mode of character representation. Porter probes the relation between money values and moral value as they pertain to masculine and feminine needs and expectations; her essay points up the weaknesses inherent in Newman's attempt to trade his cash worth for Claire de Cintré's worth as virtue's paragon.

In all of these essays, key issues recur: the clash of cultures between America and Europe; a narrative form developing from the pressure to go the way of the novel or of the romance; the art engendered by a money society; the politics of untrammeled individualism set on edge by unfamiliar social strictures; good nature opposed to malevolence; self-seeking and selfless sacrifice; aggression and passivity; wills thwarted or freely expressed; the professional moves taken by an author at a crucial stage in his career; the state of affairs in the United States of the 1870s refracted through the lens of Newman's grand transatlantic adventure in Paris; and finally, the "early James" who points prophetically to the major themes of the Master.

NOTES

1. *The Notebooks of Henry James,* ed. F. O. Matthiessen and Kenneth B. Murdoch (New York: Braziller, 1955), p. 23.
2. See the letters of James to F. P. Church of December 1, 1875, and

March 3, 1876, and of James to William Dean Howells of February 3, 1876, in *Henry James: Letters*, ed. Leon Edel (Cambridge, Mass.: Harvard University Press, 1975), Vol. II, pp. 8–9, 22–3, 31.

3. Further details of James's financial situation and the business arrangements he made to furnish essays to various journals are supplied by Leon Edel in *Henry James: The Conquest of London: 1870–1881* (Philadelphia: Lippincott, 1962), Book V, "The American," and Book VI, "A Little Journey."

4. Bibliographical data concerning the forms and editions in which *The American* appeared are from *A Bibliography of Henry James*, ed. Leon Edel and Dan Laurence (London: Rubert Hart-Davis, 1961), pp. 31–3, 87, 135, 183, 202–3, 366–7.

5. See Oscar Cargill's chapter on *The American* in *The Novels of Henry James* (New York: Macmillan, 1961) for a discussion of the possible influence upon James's novel of "L'Étrangere," the play by Alexander Dumas *fils*, which James attended in Febuary 1876. James's review of the Dumas play is contained in *Parisian Sketches: Letters to the New York Tribune, 1875–1876*, ed. Leon Edel and Ilse Dusior Lind (New York: New York University Press, 1957), pp. 84–91.

6. David Lerner, "The Influence of Turgenev on Henry James," *Slavonic Review* 20 (1941): 53.

7. Letter of May 28, 1876, from Edel, ed., *Henry James: Letters*, Vol. II, pp. 52.

8. Ibid., p. 51.

9. The following quotations taken from James's retrospective view of the time he spent in Paris between 1875 and 1876 are from Matthiessen and Murdoch, ed., *The Notebooks*, p. 26.

10. See James's letter of February 3, 1876, to Howells in Edel, ed., *Henry James: Letters*, Vol. II, p. 23.

11. Constance Rourke, *American Humor: A Study of the National Character* (New York: Harcourt, Brace, 1931), chap. 8.

12. *The American* (London: Macmillan, 1879), pp. 6–7. The Macmillan text of 1879 is the one usually preferred for readings of the "original" version of James's novel.

13. Preface to *The American*, Vol. 2, *Novels and Tales* (New York: Scribners, 1907), p. vi.

14. *A Small Boy and Others*, in *Autobiography: Henry James*, ed. Frederick W. Dupee (Princeton, N.J.: Princeton University Press, 1983), p. 30.

15. This prophetic question was raised (and answered to his seeming satisfaction) by Hector St. John de Crèvecoeur, a French immigrant to the colonies in the 1760s, in his *Letters from an American Farmer*,

written prior to the American Revolution, although not published until 1782.

16. This and the following quotations from *Notes of a Son and Brother* are from pages 419, 423–6, 449, 452–3, and 480 of Dupee, ed., *Autobiography: Henry James.*

17. Observations made in 1864 by James Jackson Jarves in his important analysis of the American "art idea" suggest relationships between the temper of the Civil War and the general nature of the culture. Jarves stated that Protestant American culture was characterized by a masculine militancy that led to the public deification of military and civic heroes. He believed that this situation made the nation's art the servant of a progressive, rationalistic, conquering, materialistic spirit – that is (as we might phrase it), of the spirit of Christopher Newman. See Jarves, *The Art Idea: Sculpture, Painting, and Architecture in America,* 5th ed. (Boston: Houghton, Mifflin, 1864), pp. 146–7.

18. Paul John Eakin, in "Reference in Biography: Henry James and the Fictions of Creativity," and James M. Cox, in "James's Trials in Autobiography" (papers presented before the Henry James Society at the 1985 Modern Language Association Convention) analyze the Portsmouth Grove scene in terms of the way it helped James to believe that he, too, was a participant in the war as a "wounded 'wound-dresser'" in order to offset the embarrassment caused by the "obscure hurt" that supposedly prevented him from entering military service. Eakin and Cox also emphasize the connections made by the older James between the young James's visit and Whitman's tending of the wounded, which appear to give James the more heroic role to play. In contrast to their approach, my concern has been to point to James's attempts to define (and to define himself in terms of) the Americanism he found vividly present at the army camp.

19. This and the following quotations are from Frederick Sheldon's "The American Colony in France," *The Nation* 26 (April 18, 1878): 257–9.

20. This and the following quotations are from James's "Americans Abroad," *The Nation* 27 (October 3, 1878): 208–9.

21. For a review of the American and British reception of "Daisy Miller," and the anger and pleasure caused by James's portrayal, see *The Woman Question: Literary Issues,* by Elizabeth K. Helsinger, Robin Lauterbach Sheets, and William Veeder, Vol. 3 of *The Woman Question, Society and Literature in Britain and America, 1837–1883* (New York: Garland, 1983).

22. Letter of October 13, 1869, to his mother, from Edel, ed., *Henry James: Letters,* Vol. I, pp. 152–3.

23. Letter of July 4, 1876, to William James, in Ralph Barton Perry's *The Thought and Character of William James* (Boston: Little, Brown, 1935), Vol. I, p. 369.

24. John Higham's *Strangers in the Land: Patterns of American Nativism, 1860–1925* (New York: Atheneum, 1981), provides an excellent historical account of the actual situation in the United States caused by the diverse population patterns introduced by the new waves of immigration that led Irving Howe to object to James's simplicity in portraying *the* American (as well as *the* American millionaire). See Howe's "Henry James and the Millionaire," *Tomorrow* 9 (January 1950): 53–5.

25. Mark Twain, "Explanatory," *Adventures of Huckleberry Finn* (New York: Webster, 1885).

26. This and the following two quotations are from *Notes of a Son and Brother*, in Dupee, ed., *Autobiography: Henry James*, p. 425.

27. Contemporary reviews of *The American* are conveniently collected in the Norton Critical Edition of James's novel, edited by James W. Tuttleton (New York: Norton, 1978). The following extracts are from *The Nation* 14 (January 11, 1877): 29; *The Galaxy* 24 (July 1877): 135–8; *Scribner's* 14 (July 1877): 406–7; *Appleton's Journal* (new series) 3 (August 1877): 189–90; *The Catholic World* 28 (December 1878): 331–4; *The Athenaeum* 2593 (July 7, 1877): 14–15; *The Academy* 12 (July 14, 1877): 33. Also mentioned is the *Atlantic Monthly* 39 (March 1877): 359–68.

28. Letter of June 28, 1877, to William James, in Edel, ed., *Henry James: Letters*, Vol. II, p. 120.

29. The critics cited here include Leon Edel, *The Conquest of London*, p. 249; Kermit Vanderbilt, "James, Fitzgerald, and the American Self-Image," *Massachusetts Review* 6 (1965): 289–304; Edward R. Zietlow, "A Flaw in *The American*," in *The Air of Reality: New Essays on Henry James*, ed. John Goode (London: Methuen, 1972), pp. 5–35; Oscar Cargill, "The American," *The Novels of Henry James* (New York: Macmillan, 1961), pp. 41–61; Cleanth Brooks, "The American Innocence," *Shenandoah* 16 (1964): 21–7; Mutlu Blasing, "Double Focus in *The American*," *Nineteenth-Century Fiction* 28, (1973): 74–84; James W. Tuttleton, "Henry James: The Superstitious Valuation of Europe," in *The Novel of Manners in America* (New York: Norton, 1974), pp. 48–85.

30. Letter of March 30, 1877, to Howells, in Edel, ed., *Henry James: Letters*, Vol. II, pp. 104–7.

31. See Robert Secor's "Christopher Newman: How Innocent Is James's American?" *Studies in American Fiction* 1 (1973): 141–153.
32. *Hawthorne* (New York: Harper, 1879), p. 43.
33. The following reviews cited here include *The Independent* 29 (May 17, 1877): 9; *The Literary World* 9 (July 1877): 29–30; *The Literary Table* 3 (August 30, 1877): 154–5; *The North American Review* 125 (September 1877): 309–15.
34. "Mr. Walt Whitman," *The Nation* 1 (November 16, 1865): 625–6.
35. Preface, *The American, Vol. 2, Novels and Tales,* pp. xiv–xvi.
36. William James to Henry James, letter of July 5, 1876, in Perry's *The Thought and Character of William James,* Vol. I, p. 370.
37. *The Eclectic* 26 (August 1877): 249–50.
38. Any study of the alterations made by James in the text of his novel is enhanced by reference to *Henry James's The American: The Version of 1877 revised in autograph and typescript for the New York Edition of 1907. Reproduced in facsimile from the original in the Houghton Library, Harvard University, with an introduction by Rodney G. Dennis* (Berkeley: Scolar Press, 1976). Royal A. Gettmann provided an important early analysis of these changes in his essay, "Henry James's Revision of *The American,*" *American Literature* 16 (1945): 279–95. The following quotations from the novel's final scene are taken from the 1879 Macmillan edition and the 1907 New York Edition.
39. The author of the piece for *The British Quarterly Review* 70 (July 1879): 141–2, initially recognized that James furthered the realism of the narrative by leaving it inconclusive at the end. "Like the experiences of life, they have no end at which we can rest; things do not get wound up, his heroes and heroines are not 'happy ever afterwards,' the end that there is is generally the reverse. His strong relentless realism leaves a large amount of failure and continuing happiness; life is left going on with many unravelled threads in its warp and woof." But having arrived at this appropriate insight, the reviewer then turns tail and complains that, as art, the novel is defective because it "leaves issues so loose and destinies so vague."
40. Robert Herrick, "A Visit to Henry James," *The Yale Review* 12 (July 1923): 724–41; Theodora Bosanquet, *Henry James at Work,* 2nd ed. (London: Woolf, 1927), p. 17; Pelham Edgar, *Henry James: Man and Author* (Boston: Houghton Mifflin, 1927), pp. 237–41.
41. Roy Harvey Pearce, "Introduction," *Henry James: The American* (Boston: Houghton Mifflin, 1962), p. xviii; William T. Stafford, "The Ending of Henry James's *The American:* A Defense of the Early Ver-

sion," *Nineteenth-Century Fiction* 18 (1963): 86–9; Royal A. Gettmann, "Henry James's Revision of *The American*"; Floyd C. Watkins, "Christopher Newman's Final Instinct," *Nineteenth-Century Fiction* 12 (1957): 85–8.

42. To cite one good example, R. W. Butterfield's essay (which notes that *The American* is James's most extensively revised narrative) points up the difference James's revisions made in his portrayal of Newman as a representative American capitalist. Butterfield finds that the 1907 version "corrects" some of the details that made the earlier Newman an unlikely accumulator of great wealth.

43. Alina Szala, "Henry James's *The American* Simplified," *Kwartalnik Neofilologiczny* (Warsaw) 16 (1969): 61–4.

44. *The Complete Plays of Henry James*, ed. Leon Edel (Philadelphia: Lippincott, 1949), p. 252.

45. Letters to Howells of October 24, 1876, and March 30, 1877, in Edel, ed., *Henry James: Letters*, Vol. II, pp. 70, 105.

2

The Turn of *The American*

PETER BROOKS

HENRY James's rereading of *The American* led him to the bemused perception that he "had been plotting arch-romance without knowing it" and that in retrospect the novel "yields me no interest and no reward comparable to the fond perception of this truth."[1] Other readers, whether or not they accept the label of romance, have been less indulgent and in particular have faulted *The American* for its apparent change of course two-thirds of the way through. Even those who are fondest of the novel have been aware that it changes radically in tone and mode at the moment of Christopher Newman's betrayal by the Bellegardes. As Leon Edel summarily states: "What happened to *The American* was that it set off in one direction – a direction that gave great pleasure to its readers – and then it sharply veered into pathos and disaster."[2] What has up to this point been largely a social comedy, broad, amused, generally good-natured, suddenly calls forth the emotional conditions and the vocabulary of melodrama, unleashing a new and heightened drama for which the reader had scarely been prepared, one that alters the very stakes of the text.

Early in chapter 18, as Newman makes his way into the Hôtel de Bellegarde: "He felt, as soon as he entered the room, that he was in the presence of something evil; he was startled and pained, as he would have been by a threatening cry in the stillness of the night."[3] With evil onstage in such overt and menacing a fashion, we may recognize that we have entered the persistent Jamesian mode of moral melodrama: a mode that may be kept in abeyance for long stretches in his fiction, held at bay by the play of social satire and urbane wit, but that most often makes its latent presence

43

felt by the time the climax is reached. What appears to make *The American* different from the later fiction is, on the one hand, the abruptness with which the melodramatic mode unfolds in the text – in so much of the later fiction, one feels its brooding presence from the start – and, on the other hand, the full specification that will be given to the melodramatic, especially to the evil that is the essential component of its menace.

"There is some foul play" (217), says Newman in chapter 18. By the time of his final meeting with Claire de Cintré at Fleurières, evil has assumed fully melodramatic lineaments. "They have bullied you, I say; they have tortured you," (241) Newman cries out; and Claire replies, "There's a curse upon this house; I don't know what – I don't know why – don't ask me. . . . I wanted to escape from it. . . . But I can't – it has overtaken and come back to me. . . . Why are there things I can't ask about – that I am afraid to know?" (242) When Claire announces her decision to "entomb" herself as a Carmelite nun, the scene unleashes all the staginess of theatrical melodrama: "The idea struck Newman as too dark and horrible for belief, and made him feel as he would have done if she had told him that she was going to mutilate her beautiful face, or drink some potion that would make her mad. He clapsed his hands and began to tremble, visibly. . . . 'You – you a nun!' he exclaimed; 'You with your beauty defaced – you behind locks and bars! Never, never, if I can prevent it!' And he sprang to his feet with a violent laugh" (243–4). Violence is confirmed as the appropriate mode for what the novel has become when, two chapters later, Mrs. Bread shows that Newman's hypothesis of "foul play" is fully justified – when she fills in the past history of the old Marquis de Bellegarde's murder by his wife, assisted by their son. The felt presence of evil has now been overtly specified, backed up by a bloodcurdling deed, which itself is documented by the deathbed note of accusation against his wife written by the old marquis and passed on to Newman by Mrs. Bread. A novel that began in urbanity and the play of worldly wit, with our introduction to Newman seated on a divan in the salon carré of the Louvre, making his first discovery of the aesthetic, seems to have veered into the gothic.

In his preface to the New York Edition of the novel, James

recognizes that there has been a "deflexion" of his fiction toward what he famously defines as "romance." He discusses what his novel might have been, perhaps should have been, had he treated the Bellegardes in terms of the "interest felt most of all in the light of comedy and of irony" (*Art*, 36). In that novel, the proud but impoverished French aristocrats "would positively have jumped . . . at my rich and easy American, and not have 'minded' in the least any drawback" (*Art*, 35). This would have given a fiction controlled by "our general sense of 'the way things happen,'" rather than the "disconnected and uncontrolled experience" of romance (*Art*, 34). Yet that novel, he continues, would not have been *The American* as originally conceived, which from its inception was committed to the idea of the "wrong" done to Newman, with his subsequently gaining access to knowledge of the Bellegardes' evil nature and past dark deeds, and thus holding them in his power. This in turn leads to James's parenthetical reflection on power as the defining characteristic of romance: "It is as difficult, I said above, to trace the dividing-line between the real and the romantic as to plant a milestone between north and south; but I am not sure an infallible sign of the latter is not this rank vegetation of the 'power' of bad people that good get into, or *vice versa*. It is so rarely, alas, into *our* power that any one gets!" (*Art*, 37).

The reflection on power cuts close to the heart of the matter, as I shall try to suggest further on. At this point, we may want to ask whether James's retrospective critique of his novel as unwitting romance really touches on the problem of *The American* as it is felt by most readers, whether it addresses itself to that change in direction noted by Edel, the swerve into "pathos and disaster." James's criterion in distinguishing between the romantic and the real is "our general sense of 'the way things happen,'" and he appears to designate as the central flaw of his text the unlikelihood of the Bellegardes behaving as such stagey villians – the much greater plausibility of their deciding to milk Newman for all he is worth. This plot, James allows, could have itself produced the "wrong" he needed, and the possession of power over others, the whole presumably in an uninterrupted vein of comedy and irony. But by stating the problem in terms of plausibility, James really avoids dealing with the change of tone and mode in his novel, its swerve toward the gothic, the sudden melodramatization of experience that to many readers, as to Edel, must appear the troublesome turn of the novel. We sense that too much of the problem is being placed on the Bellegardes' behavior, not enough on the novelist's.

But the novel in fact has not done "turning" with the introduction of the Bellegardes' betrayal, Mrs. Bread's dark revelation, and Newman's gaining of power over the villains. The gothic romance itself is transformed by Newman's final renunciation of revenge, his decision not to make use of the damning evidence put in his possession. As James retrospectively describes his original vision of Newman's final decision, "he would simply turn, at the supreme moment, away, the bitterness of his personal loss yielding to the very force of his aversion. All he would have at the end would be therefore just the moral convenience, indeed the moral necessity, of his practical, but quite unappreciated, magnanimity; and one's last view of him would be that of a strong man indifferent to his strength and too wrapped in fine, too wrapped above all in *other* and intenser, reflexions for the assertion of his 'rights' " (*Art,* 22). If with the betrayal of Newman by the Bellegardes melodrama is unleashed in the novel, in its final pages that melodrama is transmuted into the intensity of moral choice, the assertion that true melodrama is interior, that it resides in the dramas of consciousness. In this manner, *The American* distinctly prefigures James's latest fiction, perhaps most of all *The Golden Bowl,* a novel that turns on the temptation to melodrama and its renunciation, as Maggie Verver sets aside the forms of behavior "usually open to innocence outraged and generosity betrayed," and chooses instead to repair the breaking of her marriage, her trust, and her belief in the possibility of human relations, all the while experiencing the temptation to melodramatic behavior as an intensely heightened form of moral consciousness.[4] Still another fictional mode, that characteristic of James's mature "melodrama of consciousness," appears to enter *The American* in its final pages.

This evocation of how the end of *The American* prefigures the drama at the heart of *The Golden Bowl* may serve to suggest that in the turn of *The American* more could be at stake than the swerve of one novel from "comedy and irony" to melodrama. One can in fact read in *The American* and its differing modes an allegory of James's uncertain choices among different available forms of "the novelistic," his testing of them serially, and, implicitly, his search to define and create what would be the properly Jamesian form. In his preface, James indeed recognizes in *The American* an issue of mode, a question concerning the kind of novel he has written, its generic markers, the sort of reading it asks for. His bemused retrospective recognition that he "quite unwittingly" had been writing in a mode different from what he thought — that he had been "plotting arch-romance without knowing it" — may derive from a recognition that *The American* in its very texture is about various possibilities open to the novelist.

One approach to a definition of these possibilities and James's ways of choosing (and not choosing) among them might be through some of the critical terms he worked out in discussing those novelists whom he took most seriously, who seemed to him to represent viable possible models of the novel and its project. While the list of these novelists would include such English forbears as George Eliot and Jane Austen (though he is remarkably dismissive of the latter), it was really in the French novelists that he found the interesting challenges to definition of the art of the novel: particularly in Balzac, Flaubert, and Zola. In the course of his essay "Gustave Flaubert" (first published in 1902 as a preface to a translation of *Madame Bovary*), James evokes Fielding, Austen, and Pater as "instinctive and charming," and then goes on to say that "For signal examples of what composition, distribution, arrangement can do, of how they intensify the life of a work of art, we have to go elsewhere."[5] "Elsewhere" was France, where James wrote *The American,* where he had indeed settled in order to practice his art among the confraternity of those who regarded the novel as a mature and serious artistic form. That he soon became disillusioned with Paris as a place to work — and with Flaubert and his disciples as viable personal interlocutors — does not alter the fact that he continued to regard the French novelists as providing a lesson to be found nowhere else. James remains faithful to the view that the English and American novel had not really come of age, that it was still too much an entertainment for middle-class maidens, weakened by auto-censorship and a lack of self-consciousness concerning the novel as an artistic form – a proposition summarized in his well-known reply to Walter Besant, "The Art of Fiction." As he wrote to W. D. Howells in 1884 concerning Daudet, Goncourt, and Zola: "there is nothing more interesting to me now than the effort and experiment of this little group, with its truly infernal intelligence of art, form, manner – its intense artistic life. They do the only kind of work, today, that I respect; and in spite of their ferocious pessimism and their handling of unclean things, they are at least serious and honest."[6] James's judgment in this matter remains remarkably unchanged throughout his career. His valuations and critical formulations concerning individual novelists will evolve, generally toward greater sympathy and comprehension, from the early essays of *French Poets and Novelists* (published as a volume in 1878; the individual pieces had appeared in the preceding years) to those that date from the "major phase," but with enough consistency in the general problematics he discerns in each case to permit us to discuss them without worrying too much about chronology. The later essays usually mark a kind of clarification and intensification of his earlier perceptions.

James is most interested in those novelists who can teach him something about the novel, and his most important critical reflections in fact fall under the rubrics "The Lesson of Balzac" – the title of the major lecture-essay of 1905 – and the case of a Flaubert who is "more interesting . . . as a failure however qualified than as a success however explained" (*FW*, 316). For it is in his dialogue with these two major figures that we find James working out his critical positions and vocabulary. What is so surprising – and so makes of James's essays on the two writers an interesting "case" – is that despite his admiration for Flaubert's consummate artistry and his heroic effort to establish the novel as a serious artistic genre, and despite his consciousness of Balzac's artistic lapses, vulgarity, implausibilities, romantic and other claptrap, James over the years remains faithful to a perception that Balzac provides the best lesson for those who wish to recover the "wasted heritage" of the novel (*FW*, 120), whereas Flaubert, although he remains ever "the novelist's novelist" (*FW*, 329), is somehow

limited and limiting, a writer whose view of life is too exclusively
behavioristic.

We can perhaps best enter into James's dialogue with these two
masters by citing two passages, the first in praise of Balzac's respect
for the "liberty of the subject," the second criticizing Flaubert's
limiting narrative vision. On Balzac:

> There is never in Balzac that damning interference which consists of
> the painter's not seeing, not possessing, his image; not having fixed
> and held his creature and his creature's conditions. "Balzac aime sa
> Valérie," says Taine, in his great essay – so much the finest thing
> ever written on our author – speaking of the way in which the
> awful little Madame Marneffe of "Les Parents Pauvres" is drawn,
> and of the long rope, for her acting herself out, that her creator's
> participation in her reality assures her. He has been contrasting her,
> as it happens, with Thackeray's Becky Sharp or rather with
> Thackeray's attitude toward Becky, and the marked jealousy of her
> freedom that Thackeray exhibits from the first. I remember reading
> at the time of the publication of Taine's study – though it was long,
> long ago – a phrase in an English review of the volume which
> seemed to my limited perception, even in extreme youth, to deserve
> the highest prize ever bestowed on critical stupidity undisguised. If
> Balzac loved his Valérie, said this commentator, that only showed
> Balzac's extraordinary taste; the truth being really, throughout, that
> it was just through this love of each seized identity, and of the
> sharpest and liveliest of identities most, that Madame Marneffe's
> creator was able to marshal his array at all. The love, as we call it,
> the joy in their communicated and exhibited movement, in their
> standing on their feet and going of themselves and acting out their
> characters, was what rendered possible the saturation I speak
> of. . . .
>
> It all comes back, in fine, to that respect for the liberty of the
> subject which I should be willing to name as *the* great sign of the
> painter of the first order. ("The Lesson of Balzac," *FW*, pp. 131–3)

As is so often the case in James's critical essays, we have a judgment that is at once technical and somehow moral. A "respect for
the liberty of the subject" – which is shown in the novelist's giving
his created life "the long rope" for acting itself out – creates a text
in which a reader is not limited by the judgmental interference of
the novelist, where he can exercise his own freedom of discrimina-
tion: a text of pleasure, but also one that does not violate standards

for the treatment of others. Flaubert is not guilty of Thackeray's overt interferences, yet, since he was apparently "condemned to irony" – a trope that bears witness to his "comparatively meagre human consciousness" (*FW*, 336–7) – one feels that he, too, violates the liberty of the subject, showing it only in limited, controlled, and simplified form. In the following passage, James discusses the central consciousness of Flaubert's *Madame Bovary* and *L'Education sentimentale:*

> He wished in each case to make a picture of experience – middling experience, it is true – and of the world close to him; but if he imagined nothing better for his purpose than such a heroine and such a hero, both such limited reflectors and registers, we are forced to believe it to have been by a defect of his mind. And that sign of weakness remains even if it be objected that the images in question were addressed to his purpose better than others would have been: the purpose itself then shows as inferior. (*FW*, pp. 326–7)

For James, the choice of a narrative point of view that is inherently limiting and restrictive of the experience it is called upon to record constitutes a major "defect" of novelistic technique. To the objection that perhaps Flaubert wished to present such an impoverished point of view, he replies in advance that the defect then becomes one of novelistic purpose or project: It betrays a misconception of what the novel is and is for. Emma Bovary's deficiency as a character, for instance, derives from "the poverty of her consciousness for the typical function," defined as the lack of sufficient "points of contact" between her and the world (*FW*, 328).

Consider, in contrast, James's image of Balzac's "contacts" with the world: "He could so extend his existence partly because he vibrated to so many kinds of contact and curiosity. To vibrate intellectually was his motive, but it magnified, all the while, it multiplied his experience" (*FW*, 123). Despite his pretentious claims of knowledge beyond his means, then, Balzac manages to give the effect of having understood the lives of others and having given them a large stage for their enactments. Thus, where we feel an impoverishment of life in Flaubert, we everywhere sense Balzac's "spiritual presence in his work." In a summary statement, James claims: "What it comes back to, in other words, is the intensity with which we live – and his intensity is recorded for us on every page of his work" (*FW*, 127). In opposition to this intensity stands Flaubert's detached spectatorship. James writes in the essay of *French Poets and Novelists* entitled "Charles de Bernard and Gustave Flaubert": "Flaubert's theory as a novelist, briefly expressed, is to begin on the outside. Human life, he says, is before all things a spectacle, a thing to be looked at, seen, apprehended, enjoyed with the eyes. What our eyes show us is all that we are sure of; so with this we will, at any rate, begin" (*FW*, 170). Flaubert may admit that life includes as well something else "beneath and behind," but he decides that "On the whole, we will leave it to take care of itself." A lack of interest in the beneath and behind poses a significant contrast to Balzac, who is ever probing behind, to discover the latent drama and the hidden meaning – like James himself, who in the prefaces offers discussions of "going behind" and the uses of "the penetrating imagination."[7]

The nature of James's unease with Flaubert is well displayed in his stricture on the "moral" error of presenting Frédéric Moreau's beloved (but never possessed) Madame Arnoux through his limited consciousness:

> What *was* compromising – and the great point is that it remained so, that nothing has an equal weight against it – is the unconsciousness of error in respect to the opportunity that would have counted as his finest. We feel not so much that Flaubert misses it, for that we could bear; but that he doesn't *know* he misses it is what stamps the blunder. We do not pretend to say how he might have shown us Madame Arnoux better – that was his own affair. What is ours is that he really thought he was showing her as well as he could, or as she might be shown; at which we veil our face. For once that he had a conception quite apart, apart I mean from the array of his other conceptions and more delicate than any, he "went," as we say, and spoiled it. (*FW*, pp. 330–1)

James surely should not be taken to mean that Flaubert has been unfaithful to some real-life model for Madame Arnoux, or even to mean that Flaubert doesn't do justice to the "type" of the virtuous woman. He seems rather to suggest that when a novelist imagines a certain conception that has a certain potential for enactment and development, he must find the techniques of presentation that will have the effect of giving the conception that long rope necessary to its realization. To be unaware of or unconcerned with the full potential of one's created life is to be guilty of a kind of artistic totalitarianism, a lack of respect not only for life but for the high capacities of fiction to represent. If James argues that Flaubert is guilty of an error not merely technical but moral as well, it is because what is at stake for him is the very nature of the novel. Most readers would find James to be mistaken in his judgment here: They would see the limited view of Madame Arnoux presented in *L'Education sentimentale,* and indeed the antinovelistic mediocrity of "experience" in general recorded in that novel, as very much the subject of Flaubert's fiction, what it is all about. But if we want to contradict James's judgment of Flaubert, we should recognize that in his own terms he is right: He has detected that *L'Education sentimentale* is, in some radical and disquieting manner, an antinovel that undermines the very bases of the Balzacian and the Jamesian novel.

One could continue the discussion with the "cases" of Maupassant ("for M. de Maupassant himself precisely presents all the symptoms of a 'case' in the most striking way," writes James in 1888 [*FW,* 524]) and Zola: "We become conscious, for our profit, of a *case*" (*FW,* 871), James says of Zola in 1903, one that may be summarized as "the most extraordinary *imitation* of observation that we possess" (*FW,* 895), in contrast to the real thing in Balzac. The remark takes us back to a passage in "The Lesson of Balzac" where James discusses "representation" as "the most fundamental and general sign of the novel," labeling Zola's performance "an extraordinary show of representation imitated," whereas with Balzac, whatever "his faults of pedantry, ponderosity, pretentiousness, bad taste and charmless form," we sense that "his spirit has somehow paid for its knowledge" (*FW,* 130). Zola too much sacrificed to "the idea," the didactic theme each novel must demonstrate, whereas Balzac engages "the palpable, proveable world before him, by the study of which ideas would inevitably find themselves thrown up" (*FW,* 127). Representation for James always involves the "penetrating imagination" and the effort to discover the "beneath and behind." It should be neither the "behavioristic" recording of the surface of life's action nor the didactic demonstration of a conception of life.

What James so admires in Balzac — and what he finds lacking in such writers as Flaubert, Maupassant, and Zola, to the point where, in spite of their greater artistry, they have less to furnish the Jamesian novel than Balzac – may best be seized in the juxtaposition of two comments on the same incident in one of Balzac's novels, written some twenty-seven years apart. The first is from the essay of *French Poets and Novelists,* which largely praises Balzac the realist and observer and shows a certain distrust of his "visionary" streak. James particularly demurs here from Balzac's portraits of women of the aristocracy, which he labels "a laborious and extravagant failure," noting archly: "These ladies altogether miss the mark" (*FW,* 64). His decisive example concerns the incident in *Illusions perdues* where the Faubourg Saint-Germain aristocrat, Madame d'Espard, who is entertaining her provincial cousin Madame de Bargeton at the Opera, discovers that Madame de Bargeton's protégé, who calls himself Lucien de Rubempré, and who is ludicrously decked out, really is one Lucien Chardon, son of a provincial apothecary. After scolding her cousin on such an acquaintance, she sweeps out of the Opera box and goes home. "The caste of Vere de Vere in this case certainly quite forgot its repose," comments James. In the essay of 1902, James returns to this incident, as if in implicit reparation for his earlier strictures:

> The whole episode, in "Les Illusions perdues," of Madame de Bargeton's "chucking" Lucien de Rubempré, on reaching Paris with him, under pressure of Madame d'Espard's shockability as to his coat and trousers and other such matters, is either a magnificent lurid document or the baseless fabric of a vision. The great wonder is that, as I rejoice to put it, we can never really discover which, and that we feel as we read that we can't, and that we suffer at the hands of no other author this particular helplessness of immersion. It is *done* – we are always thrown back on that; we can't get out of it; all we can do is to say that the true itself can't be more than done and that if the false in this way equals it we must give up looking for the difference. Alone among novelists Balzac has the secret of an insistence that somehow makes the difference nought. He warms his facts into life – as witness the certainty that the episode I just cited has absolutely as much of that property as if perfect matching had been achieved. If the great ladies in question *didn't* behave, wouldn't, couldn't have behaved, like a pair of nervous snobs, why so much the worse, we say to ourselves, for the great ladies in question. We *know* them so – they owe their being to our so seeing

them; whereas we never can tell ourselves how we should otherwise have known them or what quantity of being they would on a
different footing have been able to put forth. (*FW*, p. 113)

James's relaxation of attitude toward Balzac's hyperbolic dramatization appears to signal a greater willingness to trust the reading
experience and the "pleasure of the text," rather than any precon-
ceived notion of representation, and a new recognition that tracing
that "dividing-line between the romantic and the real" is truly
impossible, that one cannot distinguish between the "magnificent
lurid document" and the "baseless fabric of vision," indeed that
the greatest art may be the abolition of such a distinction, the
transformation of "document" into "vision," and vice versa. He
appears to recognize that Balzac is in fact a "romantic realist," one
in whom the "directly historic" and the "romantic" – James's
terms – are never distinguishable and in whom the the representation of reality is ever subject to "those smashes of the window-
pane of the real that reactions sometimes produce even in the
stubborn" (*FW*, 113). Or as James will put it three years later in
"The Lesson of Balzac": "Balzac's great glory is that he pretended
hardest" (*FW*, 134).

The nature of that "pretending," and James's own participation
in it, are probably best expressed in the preface to *The American*,
and particularly in the celebrated passage on the "balloon of experience": "The balloon of experience is in fact of course tied to the
earth, and under that necessity we swing, thanks to a rope of
remarkable length, in the more or less commodious car of the
imagination." We might set beside this passage one from the essay
on Flaubert, where James has been describing *L'Education sentimentale* as "a sort of epic of the usual," and goes on to say: "it
affects us as an epic without air, without wings to lift it; reminds us
in fact more than anything else of a huge balloon, all of silk pieces
strongly sewn together and patiently blown up, but that absolutely
refuses to leave the ground" (*FW*, 328). In the juxtaposition of the
balloon lifting the commodious car of the imagination and the
laboriously stitched balloon that refuses to leave the earth, we
have perhaps the best possible representation of James's complex
choosing among models of the novelistic: of the apparent paradox

of his repeated declarations that the art of the novel can best be learned from Flaubert, Maupassant, Zola, all the while expressing deep reservations about their novels and declaring his unswerving allegiance to Balzac, who, despite his many lapses, remains "the father of us all" (*FW*, 120). Despite their superiority of technique, Flaubert, Maupassant, and Zola are somehow limiting and impoverishing: They do not develop the full potential of their created life, their fictions never rise to the airborne car of the imagination, there are no smashes of the window-pane. The turn that we discover in *The American* is not within their reach. And if that turn is the object of James's retrospective criticism, if he recognizes that he has played "the romancer" and "cut the cable" tying the balloon to earth, in this unintended action lies a lesson about the novelistic. If *The American* is too close to Balzac, too much a piece of romantic realism, its choice of direction nonetheless represents an important dissent from a more limiting definition of the novelistic, one out of which James would always want to smash his way.

Our sense that *The American* is a key text of James's choosing among different kinds of the novelistic derives not only from the retrospective reflections of the preface but as well from the way in which that novel itself persistently thematizes the issues and the terms James employs in his critical essays. From its outset, the novel engages us in a self-conscious process of reading, the stakes of which are concepts of freedom and the limiting restriction of freedom.[8] The initial description of Newman in the *salon carré* of the Louvre stresses the "new kind of arithmetic" represented by the aesthetic for a man whose life has been spent in American practicalities, yet stresses also that the result is "a vague self-mistrust" (17), a new look inward. Indeed, while insisting upon Newman's American identity and innocence, the description leads to a sense of his openness to new possibilities, defined as what the reader may be able to do with him as a vehicle of perception and interpretation: "Decision, salubrity, jocosity, prosperity, seem to hover within his call; he is evidently a practical man, but the idea, in his case, has undefined and mysterious boundaries, which invite the imagination to bestir itself on his behalf" (19). As a potential "register and reflector" of experience, Newman appears to be

the very opposite of Flaubert's Emma Bovary and Frédéric Moreau, whose lack of "idea," whose far too narrowly defined
"boundaries," make them limiting vehicles for the exploration of
life. They do not invite the reader's imagination to bestir itself *on
their behalf.* Newman is offered to the reader as not only interesting
in his own right – because the creation of this new "self-mistrust"
promises a drama of exploration, choice, possibly conversion – but
also as a promising optic of reading, a viewpoint on the world with
which one can do something, that will, it is intimated, sustain the
demands of the reader's imagination in the realm of the idea.
Newman offers the possibility of vision.

The possibility of vision is closely linked to the practice of freedom, which Newman, so quickly and thoroughly enriched as to be
able to turn his back on all limiting material conditions, quite
consciously represents. Newman's practice of freedom is established early in the novel, in his liberal response to the Louvre (in
contrast to Tom Tristram's suspicious bafflement), in his travels in
company with the Unitarian minister Benjamin Babcock, whose
"moral *malaise*" in dealing with European art and culture is set in
contrast to Newman's desire to "expand," the "singular inward
tremor" he derives from his tourism. If James is interested in the
adventures of the moral consciousness, here as in all his fiction, he
makes it clear from the outset that he is contemptuous of a narrow
"American" interpretation of the moral, one that excludes the
possibility of vision. But the experience of American narrowness
in the person of the unfortunate Mr. Babcock prepares the reader
for the more important and perhaps less expected contrast between Newman's practice of freedom and the limiting closure and
fixity of the world of the French aristocrats represented by the
Bellegardes.

The closure of the Bellegardes' world is advanced first in the
description of their hôtel, set in "the Faubourg St. Germain whose
houses present to the outer world a face as impassive and as suggestive of the concentration of privacy within as the blank walls of
Eastern seraglios" (50). It is a Balzacian description in that described reality is ever throwing up ideas; indeed, it insists on the
metaphoric quality of the real in ways that make it appear a self-
conscious thematization of Balzacian descriptive procedures. "The

house to which he had been directed had a dark, dusty, painted portal, which swung open in answer to his ring. It admitted him into a wide, graveled court, surrounded on three sides with closed windows, and with a doorway facing the street, approached by three steps and surmounted by a tin canopy. The place was all in the shade; it answered to Newman's conception of a convent." The foreshadowing of Claire de Cintré's eventual conventualization in the rue d'Enfer reinforces our sense that "document" is being doubled by, and made one with, the "fabric of vision." The presentation of the members of the Bellegarde clan insists upon their unfreedom, their representative fixity, their determination by assigned, inherited indentities. Madame de Bellegarde's countenance, for instance, "with its formal gaze, and its circumscribed smile, suggested a document signed and sealed; a thing of parchment, ink, and ruled lines" (120) — a sentence that both invites us to read Madame de Bellegarde as a text where the imagination has no room for play and foreshadows the damning document written by her dying husband. Claire de Cintré, on the other hand, invites our interest precisely in the drama of her possible movement from this world of fixity into one of freedom. Following Newman's proposal of marriage, "She had the air of a woman who has stepped across the frontier of friendship and, looking around her, finds the region vast" (115).

The novel will indeed develop as the struggle of fixity and freedom, most of all in the drama of Claire de Cintré's possible liberation by the American, and secondarily in the subplot of Valentin de Bellegarde and his adventure with Noémie Nioche. Valentin appears to be the freest spirit among the Bellegardes, the one who most explicitly recognizes and admires Newman's practice of freedom, who longs to start over in America, and who "derogates" from the aristocratic morgue of the Bellegardes. But Valentin will fall victim to the conventional in his liaison with Noémie, whom he regards as "a very curious and ingenious piece of machinery" (179): an attitude that denies any but a representative role — a preestablished script — to Noémie (who is only too happy to comply, to play the theatrical adventuress) and leads to Valentin's death in the most conventional of social arrangements, the duel. To Newman, Valentin's duel is a "wretched theatrical affair"

(211), and it is again theater in the mode of Valentin's and Noémie's role playing: utterly conventional, without the possibility of the free manifestation of individual potential. It is not without significance that during his watch at the dying Valentin's bedside, Newman is given a book to read, which turns out to be Choderlos de Laclos's *Les Liaisons dangereuses,* a novel about the dangerous games that can be played with conventions, in which the master of all games, the Marquise de Merteuil, describes her "pupil," Cécile Volanges, as a mere "machine à plaisir." To reduce others to machines for one's pleasure is the logical outcome of human relations based on fixed roles and closed conventions.

If the novel unfolds as the conflict of closedness and openness, of fixity and freedom, in their presentation these thematics are complicated by the fact that Newman is obliged to represent the possibilities of freedom within a context that is predetermined as fixed, conventional, set within an already written theatrical script. As Valentin says to him, his courtship of Claire de Cintré is itself a "spectacle" (107). He is forced to play a part within a genre that, by its rules and conventions, negates what his action should be. (One might meditate on what this has to do with the painful failure of the stage adaptation of *The American.*) As the novel unfolds, its presentation becomes more and more overtly theatrical, centered, in the manner of Balzac's novels, on a number of *scènes à faire,* moments where characters act out their parts on the public stage. Newman's first evening with the Bellegarde family, when he obtains permission to pursue his suit (in chapter 10), would be a good example, as would the scene of the Bellegardes' *soirée* to present Newman to their circle (in chapter 16). These are rendered in theatrical terms, with well-marked entrances and exits, bits of dramatic dialogue, various *apartés,* strong curtain lines. The scenic quality indeed is frequently made explicit by the narrator, for instance when he comments that Newman "sat by without speaking, looking at the entrances and the exits, the greetings and the chatterings, of Madame de Cintré's visitors. He felt as if he were at the play, and as if his own speaking would be an interruption; sometimes he wished he had a book to follow the dialogue; he half expected to see a woman in a white cap and pink ribbons come and offer him one for two francs" (98). If the high and broad social comedy of his scenes suggests James's fidelity to the essentially dramatic Balzacian novel, it indicates, on another level, that Newman's role as liberator is insufficient for the problem. That is, if Newman simply plays the *role* of free agent in a preordained script, he necessarily comes to be simply representative of a certain social stance. He is not, in this context, the one who can rewrite the script, break open the closure. But in fact, there will be − as in Balzac's novels − a "beneath and behind" to the stage drama, the postulation of something else that cannot be accommodated within social comedy.

There are various intimations of the latent presence of this other drama in the novel. Without giving them the detailed analysis that they deserve, we may consider the moments of explicit prefiguration of the turn impending in the novel. The first statement of it comes in ironized form from Tom Tristram, who is reacting to what he considers his wife's excessively melodramatic imagination:

> "There's Mrs. Tristram, as large as life!" cried her husband. "Observe the richness of her imagination. She has not asked a single question − it's vulgar to ask questions − and yet she knows everything. She has the history of Madame de Cintré at her fingers' ends. She has seen the lovely Claire on her knees, with loosened tresses and streaming eyes, and the rest of them standing over her with spikes and goads and red-hot irons, ready to come down on her if she refuses the tipsy duke. The simple truth is that they have made a fuss about her milliner's bill or refused her an opera-box."
>
> Newman looked from Tristram to his wife with a certain mistrust in each direction. "Do you really mean," he asked Mrs. Tristram, "that your friend is being forced into an unhappy marriage?"
>
> "I think it extremely probable. Those people are very capable of that sort of thing."
>
> "It is like something in a play," said Newman; "that dark old house over there looks as if wicked things had been done in it, and might be done again." (pp. 79−80)

The generic definition of the "play" has yet to be specified at this point: Is it comedy or melodrama? Even if Mrs. Tristram's postulate of the forced marriage stands as a valid hypothesis, the comment that this would be "like a play" distances the "wicked" event, gives it the quotation marks of irony, skepticism, or superior civilization. But we return to the idea of the forced marriage by way of Valentin's description of his sister's first marriage, to M. de Cintré, which demonstrates that the literary topos can be enacted in reality:

> "It was a chapter for a novel. She saw M. de Cintré for the first time a month before the wedding, after everything, to the minutest detail, had been arranged. She turned white when she looked at him, and white she remained till her wedding day. The evening before the ceremony she swooned away, and she spent the whole night in sobs. My mother sat holding her two hands, and my brother walked up and down the room. I declared it was revolting, and told my sister publicly that if she would refuse, downright, I would stand by her. I was told to go about my business, and she became Comtesse de Cintré. (p. 102)

The "chapter for a novel" may mark a certain gain in consistency from the "scene in a play," in that it can now figure generically in this text – a novel – as part of the history of one of its characters, recounted by an eyewitness. Together, "scene" and "chapter" in some sense legitimate Newman's own flight of fancy, in conversation with Mrs. Tristram, about the Marquise de Bellegarde:

> "Well," said Newman, "she is wicked, she is an old sinner."
> "What is her crime?" asked Mrs. Tristram.
> "I shouldn't wonder if she had murdered some one – all from a sense of duty, of course."
> "How can you be so dreadful?" sighed Mrs. Tristram.
> "I am not dreadful, I am speaking of her favorably."
> "Pray what will you say when you want to be severe?"
> "I shall keep my severity for someone else – for the marquis. There's a man I can't swallow, mix the drink as I will."
> "And what has *he* done?"
> "I can't quite make out; it is something dreadfully bad, something mean and underhand, and not redeemed by audacity, as his mother's misdemeanours may have been. If he has never committed murder, he has at least turned his back and looked the other way while someone else was committing it." (pp. 151–2)

The passage is quite remarkable in that it maintains the tone of banter and broad humor – what the narrator in the next paragraph characterizes as "the capricious play of 'American humor'" – while giving a full specification of the drama to be revealed in the coming chapters, of that turn that will make the tone of banter impossible and destroy any play of American humor. The novel here confidently predicts and assumes what many readers will take to be its self-destruction, or at least its twist to something quite unlike what it is at the moment. If James is willing to ironize melodrama and put quotation marks around the stagey, he is determined that he shall eventually have them straight as well. One could indeed say that Newman's imagination here generates the novel to come, releasing the metaphors of imprisonment that characterize the description of the Bellegardes so that they can function as metonymies: so that they can be plotted out in action. It is now the task of James's narrative to demonstrate to us that Newman has not overread the Bellegarde text, indeed that it is impossible to do so: that the Bellegardes are as bad as they appear, that the metaphoric melodrama and gothic novel they suggest really will come into being. The Bellegarde text is one that sustains the dramatic demands placed on it by the "penetrating imagination."

What follows, then, is what we have described as the novel's turn, the entry into it of the overt presence of evil, constraint, and the power of the wicked, and the creation of a nightmare predicament and atmosphere, all of this backed up by a very literal crime imparted by Mrs. Bread, documented by the Marquis's deathbed note, and entailing the further drama of Claire de Cintré's claustration and Newman's plot of revenge. If the original conflicts of the novel, thematized as closedness versus openness, fixity versus freedom, echoed James's terminology in his discussions of Flaubert and Balzac, the original terms of dramatic representation – within a prescripted social drama – seemed inevitably to favor the victory of closure and fixity. The irruption of melodrama within the text has an explosive effect on the social drama – indeed, blows it apart – and signals the victory of something closer to the Balzacian novel in one of its "smashes of the window-pane."

The way in which the melodramatic novel so abruptly displaces the novel of social comedy may indicate that James has chosen, serially or sequentially, as it were, different models of the novelistic available to him, and that he has not yet quite decided how to integrate the two. Taken together – if they can be taken together – the two parts of *The American* contain many, indeed most, of the modal elements that will define the Jamesian manner in the future. One sees in this light – in the light of our allegory of James's relation to his models – the absolute necessity of the second part, for it insists in particular – as James's fiction will continue to insist – that the social drama must live up to the demands of the penetrating imagination, that it must always, under the pressure of crisis, be ready to release its potential of melodrama. Be it the crisis of *The Ambassadors* – "a sharp fantastic crisis that had popped up as if in a dream" (II, 257–8) – or of *The Wings of the Dove* – the "Venice all of evil" unleashed by Lord Mark's visit (II, 259) – or the smashing of the golden bowl, or the burning of Poynton, or any of James's strong climaxes, we are summoned to enter a realm where the stakes have been raised, where at issue are questions of good and evil, life and death. If we do not, in the mature fiction, feel these climaxes as turns in which the novel radically changes its tone and manner, it is because the weight of the melodramatic has been felt from the beginning, in every conversation and all narratorial commentary, as part of the very style of the work. The mature work does not need the explicit prefigurations provided in *The American,* since it is constantly, and consistently, postulating the necessity for eventually entering the mode of crisis.

Yet of course – and this may mean that the implication of "immaturity" that I have been making about the novel needs to be nuanced – *The American* turns again before it is done, in Newman's renunciation of his possible revenge, in his burning of the documentary evidence of the Bellegardes' crime, in his becoming "a strong man indifferent to his strength and too wrapped in fine, too wrapped above all in *other* and intenser, reflexions for the assertion of his 'rights.' " The melodrama at the last turns inward, becomes the melodrama of the moral consciousness. And in fact, if we believe the preface, this final re-turn of the novel was present from the outset, was indeed James's original *donnée* for the novel. James describes in the preface how the idea of the novel came to him while seated in an American horse-car – much as Newman's original conversion from money making to his European venture comes to him while riding in a New York hack – and that it consisted in the idea of "the situation, in another country and an aristocratic society, of some robust but insidiously beguiled and betrayed, some cruelly wronged, compatriot'' (*Art,* 22). The interest of the situation, says James, was from the outset what the American would do in such a situation:

> He would behave in the most interesting manner – it would all depend on that: stricken, smarting, sore, he would arrive at his just vindication and then would fail of all triumphantly and all vulgarly enjoying it. . . . He wouldn't ''forgive'' – that would have, in the case, no application; he would simply turn, at the supreme moment, away, the bitterness of his personal loss yielding to the very force of his aversion. All he would have at the end would be therefore just the moral convenience, indeed the moral necessity, of his practical, but quite unappreciated, magnanimity; and one's last view of him would be that of a strong man indifferent to his strength and too wrapped in fine, too wrapped above all in *other* and intenser, reflexions for the assertion of his ''rights.'' This last point was of the essence and constituted in fact the subject: there would be no subject at all, obviously, – or simply the commonest of the common, – if my gentleman should enjoy his advantage. (*Art,* p. 22)

According to this statement, the very germ of the novel was Newman's reaction to his wrong: not the nature of that wrong but ''the interesting face presented by him to *any* damnable trick'' (*Art,* 35), that is, a situation of having been wronged that makes it possible for Newman to turn, at the supreme moment, away. This turn, which leads to the final image of Newman wrapped in those ''*other* and intenser'' reflections, thus apparently stands at the inception of the novel, which should make us realize that the turn of the novel as a whole was from the start inevitable. Indeed, it is fair to say that there was no way to get to where James, from the start, set his endpoint, in the terms of dramatization originally proposed by the novel.

That *The American* should finally appear to turn inevitably – that its turn should be into what it was to have become from the outset – may be the truly ''romantic'' element of the novel, which is largely covered up by James in the preface, where he appears to ascribe the romance element essentially to the Bellegardes' behavior. The more plausible comic fiction that he adumbrates in the preface – that of the French aristocrats jumping at the rich American – simply would not have done, in that it would not (at least as we would tend to imagine it) produce the intensified inward drama of consciousness that characterizes Newman at the end. We may speculate that this cover-up in the preface has to do with the fact — of which James may not have been wholly unaware — that what is at issue is not simply the greater or lesser consistency of *The American* — its status as romance without awareness — but the very nature of Jamesian fiction. If he misplaces the romantic label, it may be in order to conceal that the Jamesian mode, even in its maturity, is consubstantial with the romantic.

It is notable that the nature of those *"other* and intenser" reflections remains entirely unspecified. James's italicizing of *other* merely adds to its mystery, and the end of the novel itself — where Newman burns the incriminating document, then appears to show a momentary regret because of Mrs. Tristram's final remark, and turns back to the fire to find the document already consumed — does nothing to add specification to his drama of consciousness at that supreme moment. If we can in a general way guess at why Newman finds revenge ignoble and puts it aside, the text invites us to see in his gesture a formal act of closure rather than a clearly motivated moral act: "The most unpleasant thing that had ever happened to him had reached its formal conclusion, as it were; he could close the book and put it away" (306). The vague and general otherness and intensity of reflection that we are left with need to be juxtaposed to another phrase from the preface, precisely from the discussion of the definition of romance, which cannot, James argues, be reduced to the exotic: "The panting pursuit of danger is the pursuit of life itself, in which danger awaits us at every turn; so that the dream of an intenser experience easily becomes rather some vision of a sublime security like that enjoyed on the flowery plains of heaven, where we may conceive ourselves proceeding in ecstasy from one prodigious phase and form of it to another" (*Art,* 32). This appears to indicate that the novel as genre — insofar as James always defined the novel as "the pursuit of life itself" — exists to provide and to explore "the dream of an intenser experience." The novel exists to present an intensified, heightened adventure of reflection or consciousness. This is the "ecstasy" offered by fiction. The dream in which Newman wraps himself at the last is, then, generically in the nature of the novel as James conceives it. Or in other words, what Newman achieves at the very end is entry into the true world — the tone, the manner, the substance — of Jamesian fiction.

We see, then, that *The American* had to turn. For it not to have done so would have falsely imaged James's allegory of artistic intention, his choice of novelistic mode. One may want to protest that this is altogether too vague a place to end. But we must then note that the romantic element — which we now have recognized to be, in its full extension, consubstantial not only with *The American* but with all of James's fiction — stands "for the things that, with all the facilities in the world, all the wealth and all the courage and all the wit and all the adventure, we never *can* directly know; the things that can reach us only through the beautiful circuit and subterfuge of our thought and our desire" (*Art*, 31–2). The definition puts us virtually in the realm of epistemology: The romantic has to do with those things beneath and behind that we cannot know directly but that nonetheless exist by way of our thought and our desire, that become operative in life (and in fiction) to the extent that we are willing to give ourselves over to the other and intenser reflection, to pursue the dream. And fiction exists to make this other realm — what Freud described as the "other scene" of dream — imaginatively available to us. Thus the behavioristic novel must ever give way to, or be doubled by, the novel we get when we let the window-pane be smashed: when the document becomes the vision.

We may now want to recall James's parenthetical reflection that an "infallible sign" of the romantic may be the "rank vegetation of the 'power' of bad people that good get into, or *vice versa*. It is so rarely, alas, into *our* power that any one gets!" (*Art*, 37). Since so much of James's fiction appears to be a critique of power, a demonstration of the devastating effects of the manipulation of others — the denial of their freedom — one should hesitate to take this as a longing for the exercise of power over others. Is it not rather that "power" is related to "vision" and both of them to the "dream of an intenser experience"? The power associated with the romantic belongs to fiction in its ideal reach. The power of fictions enables, for example, Newman's final turning away, the "sacrifice to the ideal" that allows him to "close the book" on his adventure with the Bellegardes and to enter that reflective, retrospective dream in which the reader is supposed to accompany him. For the power of fictions is ultimately about their transmission, about how they are supposed to work upon readers. The description of this process is in some large measure what the prefaces are about, as a final retrospective rewriting of the (re)reader's meeting with the text. And we perceive by now that the critique of romance in the preface to *The American* is not the straightforward act of self-criticism it might at first appear to be. It is much more an effort to lay out a parcourse that, through the successive turns of this early novel, leads to the definition of the Jamesian novel as engaged in a melodrama of consciousness that refuses to abandon the romantic, the visionary, the panting pursuit of danger as the very stuff of novelistic representation. The very next preface of the New York Edition – that to *The Portrait of a Lady* – continues to define James's manner in its description of the novel's climactic scene, the vigil in which Isabel Archer recognizes the truth of her marriage, of Gilbert Osmond, of all that her life has become: "It is a representation simply of her motionlessly *seeing*, and an attempt withal to make the mere still lucidity of her act as 'interesting' as the surprise of a caravan or the identification of a pirate" (*Art*, 57). One senses here James's confidence that with *The Portrait of a Lady* he has achieved that fusion of the romantic and the real in the melodrama of consciousness that he always sought. The "surprise of a caravan" and "the identification of a pirate" have been transmuted into the movements of consciousness reflecting on its own choices and possibilities. This is what *The American* turns toward.

NOTES

1. Henry James, preface to *The American*, in *The Art of the Novel*, ed. R. P. Blackmur (New York: Scribners, 1934), p. 25. Subsequent references to the prefaces will use the abbreviation *Art* and will appear in parentheses in the text.
2. Leon Edel, "Afterword," *The American* (New York: New American Library/Signet Classics, 1963), p. 328.
3. Henry James, *The American*, ed. James W. Tuttleton (New York: Norton, 1978), p. 213. All of my references are to this edition – which is a

reprint of the first American book edition of 1877 – and appear in parentheses in the text.

4. Henry James, *The Golden Bowl* (New York: Scribners, 1909) Vol. II, p. 237. Subsequent references to the New York Edition (1907–9) will simply give volume and page numbers in parentheses in the text.

5. Henry James, "Gustave Flaubert" (1902) [reprinted in *Notes on Novelists*, 1914], in Henry James, *French Writers*, ed. Leon Edel (New York: Library of America, 1984), p. 333. All of my citations of James's essays on French authors are from this edition, and subsequent references will appear in parentheses in the text, using the abbreviation *FW*.

6. Henry James, *Letters*, ed. Leon Edel (Cambridge, Mass.: Harvard University Press, 1980), Vol. III, p. 28.

7. On "going behind," see the preface to *The Awkward Age*, in *Art*, p. 111; on the "penetrating imagination," see the preface to *The Princess Casamassima*, in *Art*, p. 78. For a study of Balzac's probing behind, his constant effort to discover the drama hidden behind facades and faces, see chapter 5 of Peter Brooks, *The Melodramatic Imagination* (New Haven, Conn.: Yale University Press, 1976; reprint New York: Columbia University Press, 1985).

8. On Newman as a "reader" of social codes, see chapter 2 of William W. Stowe, *Balzac, James, and the Realistic Novel* (Princeton, N.J.: Princeton University Press, 1983). On the conflict of freedom and unfreedom in the novel, see chapter 2 of Richard Poirier, *The Comic Sense of Henry James* (London: Chatto and Windus, 1960).

The Politics of Innocence in Henry James's *The American*

JOHN CARLOS ROWE

> Knowledge works as a tool of power. Hence it is plain that it increases with every increase of power.
>> — Nietzsche, *The Will to Power*

> The Republic will now be in republican hands (till now it has been managed altogether by conservatives) and we shall see how it will behave. I hope for the best. I see none but ardent monarchists and hear everything vile said about the Republic but I incline to believe in it, nevertheless.
>> — Henry James to Alice James, February 22, 1876

HENRY James's *The American* incorporates so many conventions of the novel and the romance in such a bewildering manner that critics have been understandably preoccupied with assessing the formal consequences. The "international theme" has remained just that — a theme that helps critics organize the otherwise disparate parts of a work that begins realistically, only to end with a flurry of melodramatic events. Yet, the political and historical aspects of the international theme were of considerable importance to Henry James as he began work on *The American* in the winter of 1875–6. Having ventured to become recognized as an international writer, James was personally concerned with exploring the national constraints that he would have to overcome.[1]

Choosing to live in Europe, James was attempting to overcome the narrow provincialism that he imagined had limited Hawthorne's achievement.[2] By the same token, James did not want to surrender those American qualities he considered necessary for the development of a truly international outlook. Christopher Newman is the original type of the American businessman, who is so often criticized by James for his lack of artistic sensitivity, his blunt pragmatism, and his ignorance of the psychological complexity of human relations. Nevertheless, James does not systematically criticize American capitalism in his writings, and he seems especially sympathetic to certain features of the entrepreneur in his early works. In particular, James favors Newman with a vague republicanism and a respect for work of all kinds. I am tempted to add that James also admires the ignorance of class distinctions that allows Newman to threaten the stability of such closed societies as the legitimist aristocrats of the Bellegardes' circle. Yet, it is not the *ignorance* that James admires in Newman and the American modernity he promises; indeed, it is just this ignorance that James identifies as Newman's fatal flaw. What James himself hopes to achieve as an international writer is precisely what Newman fails to achieve in Europe: the *conscious* subversion of those provincial societies (in Europe and America) that legitimate the most unnatural and arbitrary class distinctions. Such an ambition, James knows well enough, requires a thorough knowledge of both social forms and the political realities in which they are involved.

Critical discussions of *The American* customarily begin by equating Newman's innocence with his ignorance of the complex arts of European high society. Much of James's irony and social criticism focuses on the ambiguous distinction between ignorance and innocence, although the moral dimensions of this problem generally are better served in his writings by characters young enough to give some credibility to their innocence. Newman is thirty-six years old, has served in the army in the Civil War, has made a great fortune, and has had experiences as vast the American West from which he comes.[3] Roderick Hudson in *Roderick Hudson*, Isabel Archer in *Portrait of a Lady*, Hyacinth Robinson in *The Princess Casamassima*, the governess in *The Turn of the Screw*, Milly Theale in *The Wings of the Dove*, Maggie Verver in *The Golden Bowl* – these characters are much younger than Newman, both chronologically and in terms of experience. Like Lambert Strether in *The Ambassadors*, Newman is old enough to know better, which is to say that his innocence always appears to us as a slightly absurd *naiveté*.

Nevertheless, we are tempted to excuse Newman's ignorance on the grounds that he is in a foreign country. James introduces us to Newman as a caricature of the American tourist, exhausted by his efforts to comprehend the artistic sublimity of the Louvre. Marking his Baedeker, buying bad copies of masterpieces, counting the churches he has visited (he tells Valentin de Bellegarde that he has examined "some four hundred and seventy churches" in a single summer [83]), Newman is a clever parody of the tourist. For that very reason, however, he is rather endearing and sympathetic to the reader, who undoubtedly has done something similar in one country or another.

Newman's ignorance of European customs is at least initially qualified by his eagerness to "get to know the people," in the old cliché of the guidebooks. Unlike his later avatar, Adam Verver, who ships crates of European art home for his museum in American City, Newman is not a mere collector and commodifier of "experiences." Strictly speaking, Newman buys very little on his tour. In this first chapter, he buys Noémie Nioche's poor copy of Murillo's "Madonna" and then commissions her to paint an impossible number of other masterpieces, but he does so primarily to satisfy his curiosity regarding this young woman and her strange father. He also buys "a grotesque little statuette in ivory, of the sixteenth century" of "a gaunt, ascetic-looking monk" with "a fat capon hung round [his] waist" (73). As a perverse present for the morally scrupulous Benjamin Babcock, Newman's former traveling companion, the purchase gives substance to Newman's thought. In his first appearance in the Louvre, Newman seems destined to be caricatured as a gross sensualist, bent on turning every experience into a possession, with his hand always reaching for his purse. Yet, as the drama unfolds, Newman seems to use his money in subtler ways to involve himself in the lives of others: "He liked doing things which involved his paying for people; the vulgar truth is that he enjoyed 'treating' them. This was not because he was what is called purse-proud; handling money in public was on the contrary positively disagreeable to him. . . . But just as it was a gratification to him to be handsomely dressed, just so it was a private satisfaction to him (he enjoyed it very clandestinely) to have interposed, pecuniarily, in a scheme of pleasure" (197). The confusion of selfishness and generosity in this passage says a good deal about Newman's difficulties with the Bellegardes and European society in general, but it refers to a man who is by no means a vulgar tourist intent on shipping his experiences home in a trunk.

We are encouraged, then, to interpret Newman's naiveté as his unfamiliarity with European society, rather than the mere vulgarity of an acquisitive tourist or the inexperience of a raw youth. By "society," James customarily means all of the inherited forms and styles, subtle codes and postures by which a particular group maintains its authority and coherence. For the Jamesian character to enter such a group, he must first study the complicated rules of inclusion and exclusion, then attempt to imitate the behavior prerequisite to initiation.[4] For those who subscribe to such artful customs, the cost of initiation is generally the loss of individual character and the surrender to a prescribed role. Those who refuse to play by the rules and violate the necessary proprieties deliberately or unwittingly are generally exiled, killed, or otherwise sacrificed. Characters like Daisy Miller in *Daisy Miller*, Hyacinth Robinson in *The Princess Casamassima*, Milly Theale in *The Wings of the Dove*, and Charlotte Stant in *The Golden Bowl* serve primarily to expose the deadly formalism of these closed worlds. Innocent or stupid, deluded or misadvised, these characters are ultimately devices James employs to expose the hidden laws by which such societies maintain their exclusive authority.

Christopher Newman's innocence is far more complicated, however, than that of those victims sacrificed in the cause of James's social anatomies. For one thing, Newman is central to the dramatic action; he cannot be understood merely as a device to expose the Bellegardes. Unlike the relatively powerless innocents in James's fiction, Newman acts powerfully to change destinies, tempt characters with money and jobs, and offer them seemingly endless possibilities. He is not ignorant of the supersubtle psychologies of the other characters, even when he doesn't quite understand the motivations behind their behavior. Although James reminds us frequently that Newman has missed a deprecating look or a whispered joke at his expense, Newman still is conscious of significant glances, implied insults, and patronizing smiles. As much as James's narrative depends upon the interplay between what *we* are allowed to see and Newman's much more limited, subjective views and opinions, we still understand Newman to be considerably more penetrating in his psychological judgments than the conventional Jamesian naif. He misjudges Noémie Nioche, for example, but he subsequently revises his opinion on the evidence of her actions and the advice of Valentin. Although he often stereotypes other characters (M. Nioche, Valentin, the younger marquise, Lord Deepmere, and others), he is also capable of remarkably accurate first impressions of such characters as the marquis and his mother. In fact, James gives Newman a sort of uncanny prescience that often seems a function of his intuitive understanding of other characters. Shortly after he has been accepted as Claire's suitor, Newman judges the marquis and his mother for Mrs. Tristram: "I shouldn't wonder if she had murdered some one – all from a sense of duty, of course" (151) and "If he has never committed murder, he has at least turned his back and looked the other way while someone else was committing it" (152). To be sure, Newman commits many errors in judging others and misses much of what goes on around him, but he is hardly the "great Western Barbarian" that Mrs. Tristram dubs him (42).

Nevertheless, Christopher Newman is profoundly naive, primarily because he remains so fatally ignorant of the forces governing the European social circle he wishes to enter. William Stowe claims that Newman's innocence is a consequence of his failure to understand "the importance of active social intepretation for the success of his project. [Balzac's] Rastignac knows that he must fathom the secret workings of Parisian society. Newman, by contrast, is content to sit back and be amused by the antics of his foreign friends, whom he sees as performers in a great comedy of manners, actors speaking lines learned by heart and hiding their 'true selves' beneath conventional masks."[5] This strikes me as a very accurate assessment of Newman's failure, but it is just the sort of judgment that encourages readers to develop very abstract theories about appearance and reality, detachment and involvement, active understanding and passive resignation as central *themes* in James's fiction. I want to give particular concreteness to Stowe's insight by arguing that Newman's superficial observation of the Bellegardes is a consequence of his ignorance of the special role played by this family in French history and politics. Further, I shall argue that Newman's studied detachment from what the Bellegardes represent is finally part of an elaborate system of psychological defense by which Newman avoids recognizing in their aristocratic pretensions the distorted reflection of his own American identity. Newman serves James as a particular reminder that the great republican promise of the self-reliant American might end up merely repeating the rigid hierarchies of the European aristocracy. James Tuttleton economically describes the familiar problem James explored repeatedly in his international novels: "Instead of exploiting the freedom of a unique social experience to create beautiful, new, and distinctive social forms, Americans sought both to impose on the democratic New World an aristocratic social pattern developed in the Old World and, returning to the Old, to beat the Europeans on their own ground."[6] James makes it clear that such a repetition is directly proportionate to our ignorance of the political consequences of our ordinary acts. Finally, James recognizes in the secret alliances that bind together the legitimist and Ultramontanist families of the Bellegardes' circle that there are several kinds of internationalism, not all of which encourage the liberal and republican values that James himself hoped to achieve in his own project as an international modern.

Newman's ignorance of the particular psychological, cultural, and political forces governing the Bellegardes' social behavior is simply astounding when we consider how much Newman prides himself on being "current." Other than his Baedeker, "the newspapers form" Newman's "principal reading."[7] Repeatedly, James tells us of Newman's fascination with "how things were done" (55). M. Nioche combs the bookstalls for almanacs and "began to frequent another *café*, where more newspapers were taken . . . to con the tattered sheets for curious anecdotes, freaks of nature, and strange coincidences" in order to fill the French lessons he is giving Newman with the kind of timely material Newman desires: "Newman was fond of statistics . . . it gratified him to learn what taxes were paid, what profits were gathered, what commercial habits prevailed, how the battle of life was fought" (55). During his courtship of Claire, Newman "explained to her, in talking of the United States, the working of various local institutions and mercantile customs" (150–1). Yet, for all of Newman's practical American "curiosity" about how everything "works," he remains absurdly ignorant of the political situation of the family into which he plans to marry.

At the most elementary level, Newman pays little attention to the Bellegardes' religion: "He had never let the fact of [Claire's] Catholicism trouble him; Catholicism to him was nothing but a name, and to express a mistrust of the form in which her religious feelings had moulded themselves would have seemed to him on his own part a rather pretentious affectation of Protestant zeal" (246). Even after Claire has entered the Carmelite convent in the rue de Messine, Newman cannot accept the reality of a strong, committed religious vocation: "It was like a page torn out of a romance, with no context in his own experience" (276). Yet, what American traveling in Europe in 1868–9 would have been so utterly ignorant of French history as not to understand the signifi-cance of religion in any proposal of marriage into an aristocratic family like the Bellegardes?

It is not until Newman's second visit to Madame de Cintré that he asks her: "Are you a Roman Catholic, madam?" (83), even though Mrs. Tristram has already given him a precise account of Claire's religious and social backgrounds and associations (46–7). He asks this question rather idly, in the context of what appears to be a chatty conversation about the age of the house. Valentin has shown Newman the "sort of shield" above the chimney-piece that records the date 1627, and Valentin says: "That is old or new according to your point of view." Newman responds, "Well, over here . . . one's point of view gets shifted round considerably" (83). Valentin is speaking quite specifically of different political interests that might variously find their origin or end in the date 1627. At the very least, Newman ought to make some connection between this date and the early years of the Puritan Bay Colony, but even more important than this American connection are the historical events of the war waged between 1624 and 1629 by Cardinal Richelieu against the Huguenots. Richelieu attempted to exterminate the Huguenots not simply as the major Protestant opposition to Catholicism in seventeenth-century France but also as the religious basis for republican sympathies opposed to the monarchy.

Much later, Newman learns "from a guide-book of the province" that the Bellegardes' chateau at Fleurières "dated from the time of Henry IV" (237). Even so, the chateau strikes Newman as utterly "melancholy" and foreign, "like a Chinese penitentiary" (237). The date of the chateau further connects the Bellegardes with the Catholic and monarchical struggle against Protestantism and republicanism – a struggle that has particular relevance for Parisians on the eve of the Franco-Prussian War (1870–1). Henry IV protected the civil rights of the Huguenots by issuing the Edict of Nantes in 1598, but Henry's assassination in 1610 brought Cardinal Richelieu to power during the regency of Louis XIII and virtually ended all hopes of a peaceful political settlement between the Catholic monarchists and the Huguenots. Some hint of these events is given in the architecture of the Bellegardes' chateau, which has "an immense facade of dark time-stained brick, flanked by two low wings, each of which terminated in a little Dutch-looking pavilion, capped with a fantastic roof" (237). These "ugly little cupolas" suggest Henry IV's futile effort to reconcile Catholics and Protestants, because it was to Holland that many of the 400,000 Huguenots fled when they were driven out of France on the revocation of the Edict of Nantes in 1685. From Holland, of course, many persecuted Huguenots emigrated to America, where they found sympathy with other Puritans persecuted politically and religiously in Europe.

In another sense, the "little cupolas" are "ugly" because they don't "fit" the architecture of the Bellegardes' Catholic stronghold. Perhaps these architectural additions are meant to recall how the Catholics forced the Huguenots to surrender their fortified towns under the Peace of Alais in 1629. In any case, the "mixed" architecture of the chateau tells the story of the Catholic monarchists' claim to power in the stormy years of the seventeenth-century French religious wars. In her final interview with Newman, Claire explains herself only by saying, "Mr. Newman, it's like a religion. I can't tell you – I can't! . . . It's like a religion" (242). Try as he subsequently does to understand what Claire has said, Newman hasn't the vaguest idea that the connections established among religious beliefs, political positions, familial duties, and personal feelings have any bearing on Claire's ultimate refusal of him.

When these "old issues" of seventeenth century French history are discussed by critics, they are often used to associate the Bellegardes with a common theme in James's representation of the Old World. Even a critic as sensitive to historical details as John Antush places the greatest emphasis on a familiar but very general thesis about the "rise of the bourgeoisie."[8] Living in an impossibly remote past, bound tightly by anachronistic duties and obligations, the Bellegardes seem to anticipate such grotesques as Juliana and Tina Aspern, who repudiate the modern age for the sake of entombment in a dead past. Thematizing the Bellegardes in this manner, critics quickly stereotype them and neglect the immediate relevance of seventeenth-century French religious and monarchical struggles for the conflicts between monarchists and republicans, Catholics and Protestants, clericals and anticlericals at the time James was writing the novel. Like Prince Casamassima, the marquis and the old marquise are associated with reflex Catholicism, which in James's other works becomes a convenient tag for an old, impoverished, and powerless aristocracy.

The Bellegardes are by no means represented as powerless or impoverished, and they appear to be intimately involved in the contemporary political scene, even if such involvement may be defined simply by the precise forms they maintain as the signs of their particular political affiliations. The Bellegardes are not simply aristocratic Catholics; they are monarchists who resist vigorously not just the modern age but the specific politics of the republicans in the aftermath of the 1848 revolution. Their association with monarchists is even more specific: They are legitimists and Ultramontanes, as Mrs. Tristram clearly informs Newman in her first description of Claire and her ancestry (46–7). Shortly after the marquis and his mother have accepted Newman as a suitor, Newman tries to establish a more personal relation with Claire's older brother by discussing politics: "Newman was far from being versed in European politics, but he liked to have a general idea of what was going on about him, and he accordingly asked M. de Bellegarde several times what he thought about public affairs. M. de Bellegarde answered with suave concision that he thought as ill of them as possible, that they were going from bad to worse, and that the age was rotten to its core" (153). As an important representative of his class and its specific politics, the marquis is not so much offering an opinion as a formal statement. Newman's elaborate rooms overlook the Boulevard Haussmann, but Newman seems unaware of the great transformation of Paris that Haussmann directed in the ten years following Louis Napoleon Bonaparte's seizure of power from the Second Republic in 1851. The "modernization" of Paris was not merely a grand public works' project; it was an effort to consolidate Louis Napoleon Bonaparte's authority in the aftermath of the republican uprisings of 1848. The broad, straight boulevards that Haussmann designed afforded more than the long perspectives admired by Newman; they made possible much more rapid mobilization of troops in the case of popular demonstrations. Modern Paris reveals in its very architecture and urban planning the general division of classes in mid-nineteenth-century France.[9] Apparently oblivious to all of this, Newman tries to call the marquis' "attention to some of the brilliant features of the time," without realizing that such "brilliance" more likely than not would only sharpen the marquis' sense of his embattled position as a monarchist of the old school.

On the evidence of Newman's apparent innocence of the political issues involved, the marquis makes a very direct statement: "The marquis presently replied that he had but a single political conviction, which was enough for him: he believed in the divine right of Henry of Bourbon, Fifth of his name, to the throne of France" (153). Newman is neither "horrified nor scandalised, he was not even amused" by this declaration, but "after this he ceased to talk politics with M. de Bellegarde." James makes it clear that Newman considers such views the quaint reminders of a distant past with no relevance for the present: "He felt as he should have felt if he had discovered in M. de Bellegarde a taste for certain oddities of diet; an appetite, for instance, for fishbones and nutshells. Under these circumstances, of course, he would never have broached dietary questions with him" (153). What is particularly remarkable is the degree to which Newman judges such views to be peculiar personal idiosyncrasies, like dietary habits.

Nevertheless, the Bellegardes belong to a very well defined and active political minority in nineteenth-century France. As *legitimists*, the Bellegardes support the royal claims of Henri Charles

Ferdinand (1820–83), who styled himself Henry V and was the legitimist pretender until his death. The younger Bourbon line of the House of Orléans had come to power during the Revolution of 1830 when Louis Philippe (1773–1850) was named king by the revolutionaries after Charles X had been deposed. Louis Philippe was himself deposed in the Revolution of 1848, but the Orléanists' claim to power was maintained by a succession of pretenders between 1848 and 1873, when Louis Philippe Albert (1838–94), the grandson of King Louis Philippe, relinquished his claim to the throne in favor of the legitimist pretender, Henri Charles Ferdinand, known as the Comte de Chambord as well as Henry V.

The controversies between the legitimists and the Orléanists in the period following 1848 turned primarily on the more general disputes between clericals and anticlericals in the nineteenth century. The Orléanists had already made a shaky alliance with the republicans in the Revolution of 1830, but the legitimists remained stubbornly opposed to any reconciliation with republican or liberal politics. Unlike the Orléanists, the legitimists worked to build an international power base centered in the pope's temporal and spiritual authority in Rome. They aligned themselves with (and were often the same as) those *Ultramontanes* ("beyond the mountains" – referring to Rome as their ultimate authority) working in the nineteenth century to protect the temporal power of the papacy, dreaming of a Europe united along the lines of the ancient Holy Roman Empire and under the papacy's absolute sovereignty.

Although there is no specific evidence associating the Tristrams with Orléanist circles, there is a strong sense in the novel that the Tristrams and Bellegardes belong to very different social sets. Customarily, this social distance, especially between the old school friends, Claire and Lizzie, is explained in terms of the extremely exclusive aristocratic order of the Bellegardes and the relative modesty of the Tristrams' social connections. Tom Tristram is so self-indulgent as to make any attempt to connect him with politics seem ludicrous. Nevertheless, he fits almost perfectly the type of American expatriate James describes in several contemporary letters in the following manner: "A type I have little esteem for is the American Orleanist of whom I have seen several specimen [sic]. Of all the superfluous and ridiculous mixtures it is the most so."[10]

There is at least the hint, then, that the Tristrams are associated with those Orléanists who sought alliances with French republicans and foreign democrats. Needless to say, the Bellegardes would hold the frivolity of such "allies" in considerable contempt, and rightly so in James's view.

The French republican revolution of 1848 spread liberal, anti-Bourbon sympathies to Germany, Austria, and Italy. The ducal line of Bourbon-Parma and the royal line of the Two Sicilies connected the French Bourbon legitimists with imperial claims in Spain and Italy as well as with the Holy See. The Italian Risorgimento focused republican antagonism against the Catholic Church and the Bourbons, notably in the famous expedition of Garibaldi's One Thousand that overthrew the Bourbon government of Sicily and Naples in 1860. Between 1860 and 1870, Pope Pius IX (r. 1846–78) was continually under siege from republican Italian troops intent on reclaiming papal territories in Italy. Only the French troops sent to Rome by Napoleon III prevented Pius from being utterly stripped of his temporal power until 1870, when France's losses in the Franco-Prussian War (notably the Battle of Sedan) forced the withdrawal of its troops from Rome.

Valentin tells Newman early in the novel: "The only thing I could do was to go and fight for the Pope. That I did, punctiliously, and received an apostolic flesh-wound at Castelfidardo. It did neither the Holy Father nor me any good, that I could see. . . . I passed three years in the Castle of St. Angelo, and then came back to secular life" (93). Valentin's bitter irony says a good deal more about the political situation in Europe than Newman comprehends. In the first place, Valentin served the pope with the Zouaves, mercenaries recruited from among French soldiers in Rome in 1860, under General L. C. Léon Juchault de Lamoricière, to serve as personal defenders of the pope. On August 28, 1860, Italian republican ambassadors requested Napoleon III's permission to invade the Papal States, which separated the northern states, unified in April as "Victor Emmanuel's kingdom," and the Kingdom of Naples to the south, where Garibaldi's forces were fighting the Bourbons. "Bonne chance, mais faites vites," Napoleon III was reputed to have told them, acknowledging that his permission was a betrayal of legitimist interests in France. Only a quick Italian victory might save the French emperor from the possibility of growing opposition at home. The Piedmontese army moved south, encountering only pockets of resistance from the papal army. The only significant clash in this first advance occurred in the small village of Castelfidardo on the Adriatic coast. The military annexation of the Papal States, together with Garibaldi's military successes in the south, marked the beginning of a genuinely unified Italy and the virtual end of the pope's temporal authority in Europe.[11] It is little wonder that the duchess and others in the Bellegardes' circle trade stories about snubs or insults given to "the great Napoleon" (290). Undoubtedly Napoleon III of the Second Empire is the object of their abuse, since he had helped precipitate the collapse of Bourbon and papal power with one swift decision. Only a year after the end of the action of *The American*, in 1870, the Zouaves in Rome would be overrun by Italian troops, thus concluding formally the pope's rule of any political territory in Europe, except for the one square mile granted him as Vatican City. Mobilized for action in the Franco-Prussian War, the Zouaves were disbanded after the French surrender to the Germans in 1871. Thus Valentin is associated not merely with the battlefield and a dying aristocracy, as critics have been fond of noting; he is associated with the sharp blows to legitimist hopes that accompanied the Italian Risorgimento. The embattled position of the French legitimists is in some measure reflected by the situation of the Catholic church. While the republican troops invaded Rome, the ecumenical council was meeting to publish that monument to the church's defensive position in the nineteenth century, the Dogma of Papal Infallibility, issued in 1870.

I can hardly hope to reconstruct here the complex history of the legitimist supporters of the Bourbon line in the stormy years of European history following the Revolution of 1848, but these familiar details of that history should suggest that the legitimists' concerns about their vanishing political power in France, their stubborn resistance to alliances with republicans (variously negotiated in the same period by Orléanists), and their vain hope of establishing an international power base that would restore papal rule of Europe have considerable relevance for Newman's little romance in the winter of 1868–9. Only one year later, France would go to war with Germany primarily over the threat of a Hohenzollern assuming the Spanish crown and thus surrounding France to the east *and* the south with Prussian rule. Yet, the political concerns fueling the Franco-Prussian War went considerably beyond the military jeopardy posed to France by a Prussian's accession to the Spanish throne. In the minds of many Frenchmen, the idea behind this political maneuvering was the Austro-Germanic dream of reviving the old Holy Roman Empire under German and *Protestant* authority.

In the midst of these ongoing power struggles and on the eve of open hostilities between France and Germany, the Bellegardes represent an embattled political force in contemporary France. In the letters Henry James wrote for the *New York Tribune* between 1875 and 1876, while he was working on *The American*, he pays special attention to the effects of political life in Paris on the arts and high society. As Leon Edel notes, the *Tribune* "was not relying upon James for its French news coverage; for that it had the seasoned William H. Huntington, and for political stories it could also call upon the services of John Paul. James was free to deal with whatever struck his fancy in the Parisian scene."[12] Even so, James begins many of his letters (especially the first nine or so) with fairly detailed accounts of political events. Familiar with legitimist opposition to the newly elected republican majority, he calls repeatedly for liberal toleration of this and other conservative minorities in France. The abortive republican commune of 1870, provoked by Napoleon III's disastrous losses in the first stages of the Franco-Prussian War, had resulted in a conservative backlash at the end of the war. The National Assembly of 1871 was Catholic and royalist, and the Bourbon pretender, Henry V, was very nearly restored to power.

The return of republicans to political power during James's year in Paris brought with it a particularly vehement liberal anticlericalism. The rapid changes in the political revenge drama acted out in France after the Franco-Prussian War have certain similarities to the cycles of revenge that organize the plot of *The American*.[13] Throughout the nineteenth century, Catholics had struggled to maintain the freedom of their schools; freedom of primary teaching had been granted them in 1833 and freedom of secondary teaching with the Failloux Act of 1850. But republican fears of a legitimist restoration of the Bourbon monarchy in the 1870s fueled an anticlericalism that focused on the freedom of Catholic education in France.

Léon Gambetta (1838–82) was a political moderate, except in his vigorous opposition to the Ultramontanes and legitimists. In his letters for the *Tribune*, James criticizes Gambetta's opposition to the Catholic University – that is, opposition to the toleration of Catholic education at the university level. We ought to recall that the Hôtel de Bellegarde is located in the rue de l'Université. This is an important street in the aristocratic neighborhood of the Faubourg St.-Germain, but James's selection of it may well be intended to evoke the current clerical and legitimist claims for the freedom of Catholic universities. In his letter of March 4, 1876, James writes:

> M. Gambetta has just been making an eloquent speech at Lille. . . . It is all very reasonable as well as eloquent, save in so far as it commits the liberal program to antagonism to the new Catholic University. M. Gambetta denounces in violent terms the admission of the Church to a share in the superior instruction. This is a point on which many sagacious Republicans distinctly differ with him. . . . If I were a Frenchman I am inclined to think that I should feel more at my ease in a republic in which the Catholic party was allowed to carry on, in competition with the Sorbonne and the Collège de France, as successful and satisfactory a university as it could, then in a republic in which it was silenced and muzzled and forced to disseminate its instruction through private channels. It is hard to imagine a Catholic university, with the full light of our current audacity of opinion beating down upon it, proving very dangerous. (*PS*, p. 75)

Leon Edel suggests that James's "typically American point of view" in this passage prevented him from fully understanding "how much more difficult such a question was in a context of European politics than of American" (*PS*, 177). In particular, Edel notes how the Catholic University issue is linked with the larger claims by legitimists and Ultramontanes for an authority outside France: "The Church was not only competing in the matter of education, but was trying to make France the defender of papal interests against the new Italian kingdom and against Bismarck's

Kulturkampf in Germany" (*PS,* 177). James's proposal for republican toleration of Catholic legitimists is not as self-evidently naive as Edel suggests, although it certainly betrays a rather idealistic faith in the model of American democracy at this early stage in James's career. James confidently assumes that a free democracy defends itself best by granting freedom of speech to those minority views that challenge the ruling government. James concludes that such a "free" exchange in France would prove the superiority of the republicans' liberalism over the Catholic legitimists' narrower concerns. It is also possible that James understood how much more dangerous repressed minorities can be to a government than those openly tolerated. Republican persecution of the legitimists and clericals *did* drive them into foreign alliances that were not in the best interests of the French nation. Indeed, the secrecy and exclusiveness of the legitimists have some affinity with the secrecy and privacy of the Bellegardes in *The American.* James's position regarding the Catholic University issue expresses his commitment to open political debate and the citizen's right to be informed of all conflicting views in order to make intelligent political choices.

Above all, James shows his knowledge of the contemporary political situation in France and Europe in his letters for the *New York Tribune.* Newman remains blithely unaware of the effects of these historical and political events on his own destiny. Newman never understands that his proposal to Claire de Cintré is from the beginning a political act. When Newman proposes a fete in his apartments on the Boulevard Haussmann to celebrate his engagement, he is attempting to force the Bellegardes to acknowledge publicly his acceptance by the family. Newman attributes their reluctance to publicize the engagement merely to their personal snobbery; he never reflects upon the political significance that would naturally attend the announcement by an important legitimist family of its alliance by marriage with an American democrat. Coerced by Newman's political blundering into hosting the party at the Hôtel de Bellegarde, Madame de Bellegarde must realize that she is publicizing and giving social credibility to the marriage of a vaguely Protestant American to the daughter of committed Catholic legitimists. Valentin remains sufficient evidence that a number of legitimists, especially those who had fought for the pope in Italy, were disillusioned with the ultraconservatism of their kin and inclined to reach some accord with the republicans. As the Risorgimento reduced the Bourbon and papal powers between 1860 and 1870, many legitimists must have given up their international cause for more practical alliances.

Deprived of power as a younger son, unrewarded for his military service, the dilettantish Valentin is a likely candidate for reconciliation with the republicans. Valentin seems merely "curious" to see what Newman's proposal to Claire will bring about, much in the manner of Mrs. Tristram's personal curiosity. Nevertheless, he is careful to warn Newman about the family's history – "we are eight hundred years old" (109) – and to insist that Newman's "success will be precisely in being to her mind, unusual, unexpected, original" (108). When Valentin does agree to accept Newman's suit, he seems at first to do so according to Newman's very commercial habit of making a verbal contract. Yet, Valentin's offer of his hand to Newman has much more the character of a political or military alliance: "'*Touchez-là,* then,' said Bellegarde, putting out his hand. 'It's a bargain: I accept you; I espouse your cause'" (109). He adds that he does so not only because he likes Newman personally but because "I am in the Opposition. I dislike someone else" (109). There is no reason to assume that Newman's guess, "Your brother?" isn't correct, but it might just as well be Henry V or Pope Pius IX or virtually any other significant representative of legitimist and Ultramontanist claims to authority. Understood in that political context, Valentin's brother might certainly be hateful in terms of the frustration his party has caused Valentin.

There is considerable evidence to support the speculation that the Bellegardes have agreed to Newman's suit as much for its political significance as for the financial advantages he brings. This hypothesis admittedly does not bear the scrutiny of James's remarks on the Bellegardes in his 1907 preface to the New York Edition of *The American*. In a less romantic version, in a thoroughly realistic mode, the Bellegardes "would positively have jumped then . . . at my rich and easy American, and not have 'minded' in the least any drawback" (12). Nevertheless, the older and more skeptical James of 1907 concludes that "such accommodation of the theory of noble indifference to the practice of deep avidity is the real note of policy in forlorn aristocracies – and I meant of course that the Bellegardes should be virtually forlorn" (12). Yet in this judgment, James in 1907 simply may not be recalling very well his own youthful idealism. The Bellegardes are hardly represented in the 1877 edition of the novel as "virtually forlorn," either in terms of financial means or political influence. They may have lost much of their ancestral authority, but their behavior betrays little of the desperation of those later aristocrats in James's fiction who preserve only the scantest tokens and ribbons of nobility.

Perhaps James's more skeptical twentieth-century views of the European aristocracy reflect something of his own development as a social critic, as well as the changes in European history since 1875. In any case, the difference between James's representation of the Bellegardes' dignity and "grit," to say nothing of their relatively comfortable circumstances, in the first edition of the novel and in his more evident contempt for "forlorn" aristocrats in 1907, may account for the substantial revisions he made in the version prepared for the New York Edition. This change in James's views – and biographical matters would seem to support such a change – gives further warrant to those critics who contend that the two editions constitute two different novels.[14] In any case, the argument for the political allegory in *The American* is shown to its best advantage in the first edition, which remains the closest to the particulars of Parisian politics that James was observing firsthand.

When Newman approaches the old marquise to receive her approval of his marriage suit, he finds her in the company of the old Comte and Comtesse de la Rochefidèle. Indeed, a reading of *The American* as political allegory gains considerable support from the tag names James uses for the legitimist aristocrats: Rochefidèle, Grosjoyaux, d'Outreville, Lord Deepmere, and others. Many of their names refer to natural objects or places that would give some tonal legitimacy to their right to rule. Madame de Bellegarde introduces Newman by saying: "I have been telling Madame de la Rochefidèle that you are an American. . . . It interests her greatly. Her father went over with the French troops to help you in your battles in the last century, and she has always, in consequence, wanted greatly to see an American" (145). The comte tells Newman: "Monsieur is by no means the first American that I have seen. . . . Almost the first person I ever saw . . . was the great Dr. Franklin. . . . He was received very well in our *monde*" (146). Newman responds in no way to these remarks, which he apparently takes for idle social chatter. Yet, the very presence of the Rochefidèles on the planned occasion of the Bellegardes' acceptance of Newman's suit argues for some premeditation and design. On the one hand, we might speculate that the Rochefidèles are merely speaking defensively and thus justifying their tolerance of democrats like Franklin. On the other hand, they may be suggesting, much more significantly, that an alliance of legitimists and Ultramontanists with American republicans might help these embattled aristocrats gain even more international support for their battles within France. Indeed, an alliance with that paradoxical democratic type, the American millionaire, might well be viewed by some legitimists as a gain in financial and political power that would offer an acceptable compromise to those urging reconciliation with the proletarian republicans of 1848.

Critics intent on viewing *The American* as James's first major transformation of the romance into his own brand of realism are fond of discussing Newman's "education" from innocence to disillusioned knowledge. R. W. Butterfield's argument is representative: "It should be noted that *The American* changes character, as Newman's vulnerable naïvety develops into a self-protective awareness. It begins as a novel that is 'realistic' in its social observation and narrative material, yet one that is seen chiefly through the eyes of a man who has a 'romantic' (and thus, in some sense, false) vision of Europe, a vision altogether too benign and 'innocent'. It concludes as a novel in which melodramatic and 'romantic' events (duels, dark secrets, devilish glances, murders, flights into convents) expose the 'reality' of Europe, which Newman now sees, in all its thickness and complexity of history and evil, beneath the deceptive surface of appearances."[15] Yet, Newman's consistent ignorance of French politics and history supports another view: that Newman's fatality is his utter failure to turn his experience into any kind of instructive or useful knowledge.

Even the fortune Newman has amassed confirms this judgment of his lack of education. Critics hunt about for clues to the real basis for Newman's fortune: washtubs, leather, cooper, railroads, the stock market? Newman is as much a dabbler in these commercial fields as Tristram is a social dilettante; neither respects the material he works and the product he makes. No idea transcending immediate appetites takes any firm hold in either man's mind. This helps explain why Newman's desire for some such idea results in nothing more significant than his romantic idealization of himself projected onto the screen of a twenty-four-year-old French woman, who is herself neither particularly beautiful nor accomplished. Newman's "idea" is as childishly selfish as the story Claire reads to her niece, Blanche, "Florabella and the Land of the Pink Sky." To the bitter end, Newman remains convinced of his goodness, generosity, and honesty, just as Tom Tristram maintains his buoyant "good nature" in all weathers. There are many different, often deceptive "ideas" that will wreck James's subsequent characters, but the idea that Newman lacks still has some attractions for the young James. *The* idea that transvalues selfishness into self-consciousness always involves some conception of involvement in a larger and more enduring community. There can be no proper marriage between Claire and Newman until there is some idea of a social responsibility that will transcend the self and the family.

In his zeal for revenge against the Bellegardes, Newman visits the duchess, Madame d'Outreville, that planted presence who attracts such worshipful attention from the aristocrats at the Bellegardes' fateful ball. In her conversation with Newman, she "talked to him about flowers and books, . . . about the theatres, about the peculiar institutions of his native country, about the humidity of Paris" in what strikes Newman as nothing so much as the idle twaddle of a powerless leisure class. By the same token, we might speculate that the tangle of "social" subjects in the duchess's conversation reflects James's own conviction that social, personal, political, and philosophical issues are all part of the same "conversation," but such an insight is lost on Newman: "And then as the duchess went on relating a *mot* with which her mother had snubbed the great Napoleon, it occurred to Newman that her evasion of a chapter of

French history more interesting to himself might possibly be the result of an extreme consideration for his feelings" (290).

Interrupted by the arrival of an Italian prince, Newman is asked by the duchess to remain. The duchess's conversation with this prince is explicitly political and thus more difficult for Newman to personalize:

> She made a fresh series of *mots,* characterised with great felicity the Italian intellect and the taste of the figs at Sorrento, predicted the ultimate future of the Italian kingdom (disgust with the brutal Sardinian rule and complete reversion, throughout the peninsula, to the sacred sway of the Holy Father), and, finally, gave a history of the love affairs of Princess X⎯⎯. . . . The sentimental vicissitudes of the Princess X⎯⎯ led to a discussion of the heart-history of Florentine nobility in general; . . . and at last declared that for her the Italians were a people of ice. (pp. 290–1)

Newman senses "a sudden sense of the folly of his errand. . . . The duchess . . . had built up between them a wall of polite conversation in which she evidently flattered herself that he would never find a gate" (291). The duchess and the Italian prince are engaging in a polite but nevertheless significant discussion of European politics. The "sentimental vicissitudes of the Princess X⎯⎯" have as much to do with the Bourbon claims to European rule as Italian military exploits against the Bourbons in Sicily and their annexation of papal territories. Given the entanglement of noble family genealogies and political issues in European history, there is every reason to suppose that the flirtations of a princess may have as much political significance as a military coup. Newman, together with many modern critics, assumes that Urbain de Bellegarde's work on his history of "The Princesses of France Who never Married" simply represents the ascetic ideals of a dying aristocracy. Yet, the aristocrat's obsession with family genealogies had very specific political importance. Any political group supporting a pretender to the throne, particularly one who claims his divine right to rule, has some special interest in royal families' genealogies. The barrier that separates Newman from the duchess and the prince is certainly determined by different hereditary classes and cultures, and we have no reason to suppose that James finds these ultraconservative aristocrats any more attractive for all of Newman's ignorance. It is also a wall that continues to divide the personal from the social, the subjective impression from the historical event for Newman. The duchess may well be putting Newman off with her endless banter, perhaps in deference to her friends and allies, the Bellegardes. On the other hand, it is possible that she is teaching Newman a little lesson about the necessary entanglements of social and political concerns in her *monde.*

To the end of his story, Newman continues to ignore or repress the political realities of European aristocratic society. The romance and melodrama that he composes out of the unacceptable fact of his rejection by these legitimists is quite evidently a defensive effort to contain and neutralize the power they have wielded over him. He treats the Bellegardes in much the same manner as he treats Urbain's apparently frivolous wife, the young marquise, and as he treats Claire and Valentin: helpless children in need of his paternal care. Yet, in this paternal role, he is blinder to the power these "children" wield over him than M. Nioche is of the machinations of his daughter, Noémie. Indeed, the curious crossing of the apparently farcical subplot of the Nioches with the larger drama involving Newman and the Bellegardes suggests something of Newman's enduring ignorance of the bare events of the world he has entered. Repeatedly, Newman tells Claire that he will make her "safe," be a "father" to her, and thus paradoxically give her complete "freedom" (163–4). Yet, James understands that democratic freedom comes only from a full awareness of the different and often conflicting political choices that citizens are required to make. Thus James endorses the right of the Catholic legitimists to be represented in a free democracy such as he hopes will come from the republican majority in the Assembly of 1875–6. All of Newman's patronizing sexism and patriarchal condescension to women is involved in his utter ignorance of contemporary European politics and past history. Having divided polite society from commercial and political concerns, Newman assumes that a *woman*'s grandest ambition is to wield maternal power like Madame de Bellegarde's. His attitudes toward women are at least as reactionary as those of this small aristocratic circle into which he has blundered.

Newman's paternalism is, of course, linked with his naive understanding of "self-reliance" as an individualism that carries with it obligations only to oneself and the immediate family that is its patriarchal extension. Never does Newman wonder about the political responsibilities of the self in its various manifestations as son, daughter, businessman, aristocrat, father. He views poor old M. Nioche as a deluded and hypocritical man, manipulated against his shattered will by a daughter who uses her arts to rise in the world. The story that the Bellegardes circulate about Valentin's death in his sordid duel with Mr. Stanislas Kapp is explained by Lord Deepmere: "They got up some story about its being for the Pope; about the other man having said something against the Pope's morals. . . . They put it on the Pope because Bellegarde was once in the Zouaves. But it was about *her* morals — *she* was the Pope!" (300). By the same token, *Claire* is the pope, especially in her withdrawal into the Carmelite convent in the rue d'Enfer. The story told by the Bellegardes about Valentin may be strictly false, but it suggests how every social relation carries with it significant political consequences.

Valentin dies in a duel with Mr. Stanislas Kapp, the son of a German brewer, in a way that seems to speak only of the disappearance of an anachronistic class incapable of changing to meet the new age. Prompted by a trivial romantic triangle, the duel farcically anticipates the absurd national "honor" for which France nominally entered the Franco-Prussian War.[16] But to James, Valentin's absurd gesture seems preferable to Newman's utter ignorance of how politics and high society work together. Valentin consciously *chooses* his vain destiny, even down to the second shot he fires deliberately wide of its mark. Newman chooses nothing but ignorance, willfully repressing the larger political issues that might well have caused the Bellegardes to command Claire to break her engagement with Newman. The romance that Newman finally "closes" as he stares at the blank walls of the convent in the rue d'Enfer has been constructed by Newman out of this willful blindness.[17]

Yet, it is not just Newman's ignorance of history and politics that frightens James in his treatment of the modern American. Above all, James recognizes how easily this "new man" might serve the old causes. Ignorance is always an obedient servant. James's concern that the American new man might well become just another version of the arbitrary European ruler, all the while professing the most democratic sentiments and in full confidence of his own good will, adds special force to the political allegory I have sometimes forced upon *The American*. It is just Newman's paradoxical combination of aristocratic self-reliance and democratic appearance that might make him a reasonable candidate for marriage into a French legitimist family.

Throughout *The American*, Newman's political ignorance serves as a measure of his failure to recognize *himself* in any of the characters he encounters, including the imaginary "Claire" he constructs in his own image. The superficiality of his *perceptions* and *impressions* involves not only his political ignorance – that is, the extent to which history underlies every apparently direct impression or observation. It also involves his studied refusal to recognize his own paternalism in the Bellegardes' imperious authority over Claire, his own hypocrisy in M. Nioche's surrender to his daughter's ambitions (are these any worse than Newman's prospective service in the political ambitions of the Bellegardes?), his own passion for revenge and violence in the Bellegardes' implied murder of the old marquis. It is in this final respect that Newman's supposed education is so utterly deficient by Jamesian standards.

In this last regard, we must recall what drove Newman to Europe in the first place: "I had come on to New York on some important business . . . a question of getting ahead of another party, in a certain particular way, in the stock-market. This other party had once played me a very mean trick. I owed him a grudge, I felt awfully savage at the time" (34). Newman's ride in his "immortal, historical hack" provokes that "sleep" or "reverie" from which "I woke up suddenly . . . with the most extraordinary feeling in the world – a mortal disgust for the thing I was going to do" (34). Many critics speculate that Newman repeats this gesture of cathartic renunciation when he burns the incriminating note and gives up his revenge against the Bellegardes. As I have argued, however, Newman's first decision to throw revenge over occurs not when he dramatically burns the note in Mrs. Tristram's grate but when he visits the duchess. There he surrenders before the impenetrable wall of her conversation. It is the same figurative wall Newman will contemplate much later in the rue d'Enfer – not just the "blank wall" of Claire's withdrawal from the world, but the wall of Newman's ignorance of those political realities — those larger ideas — that bind the duchess, the Italian prince, and the Carmelite sisters to the same social will.

For after all, when faced with "mortal disgust," Newman flees both the situation and himself. Those who would contend that Newman maintains his integrity from the beginning to the end of the romance need to be reminded that repetition is proportionate to repression. Newman has never come to terms with that mortal disgust he could experience only involuntarily in his sleep or reverie, but that tells only part of his final story. The doubling of these two significant moments of renunciation helps bring America and Europe closer together insofar as both New World capitalism and Old World aristocratic politics may have more in common than first meets the eye.

The political interpretation of the Bellegardes' willingness to marry Claire to Newman adds an interesting perspective to this argument. Perhaps the international aims of American capitalism are, for James, potentially more kin to the internationalism of French legitimists and Ultramontanes than to James's own republican ideals. *The American* may well be a subtle warning to James's readers, as well as to James's own literary ambitions, that the international destiny of the self-reliant American may have more in common with the imperial claimants of France (the Bellegardes), England (Lord Deepmere), and Italy (the ducal line of Bourbon-Parma, the pope) than we in our democratic enthusiasm are willing to admit. Given the intense concentration in his subsequent works on the special consciousness of imaginative and willful characters, James was right to express some concern that such "fine consciences" not be mistaken for a new aristocracy, as intent upon securing its power by international means as today's heads of multinational corporations.

NOTES

1. I make the argument for James's conscious bid to become an international in *The Theoretical Dimensions of Henry James* (Madison: Univer-

sity of Wisconsin Press, 1984), pp. 30–57. I have written a companion piece to the present essay, which explores the psychological aspects of Newman's political and historical ignorance in *The American:* "The Politics of the Uncanny: Newman's Fate in *The American,*" *The Henry James Review* 8 (Fall 1987), forthcoming.

2. Henry James, Jr., *Hawthorne* (New York: Harper and Brothers, 1879), p. 42: "If Hawthorne had been a young Englishman, or a young Frenchman of the same degree of genius, the same cast of mind, the same habits, his consciousness of the world around him would have been a very different affair; however obscure, however reserved, his own personal life, his sense of the life of his fellow-mortals would have been almost infinitely more various."

3. For reasons discussed later in this essay (see note 14), I am using the first edition of *The American* rather than the much revised New York Edition. Because James Tuttleton's Norton Critical Edition of *The American* (New York: Norton, 1978) uses the more authoritative London Macmillan edition of 1879 as a copy text, but records all variants between the Boston edition of 1877 and the London edition of 1879, I have chosen to use the Norton edition as an authoritative text for a study of the "first edition" of *The American.* All page references are included in the text.

4. Manfred Mackenzie in *Communities of Honor and Love in Henry James* (Cambridge, Mass.: Harvard University Press, 1976) provides brilliant structural analyses of these rites of inclusion and exclusion in James's fictional social worlds. À propos of Newman's transformation of his ignorance of history and politics into his own private melodrama in *The American,* Mackenzie's following remarks are especially helpful: "If the Jamesian hero's quest for identity and honor implies another or a second go, then his story may very well take a one-two form. Insofar as this hero quests compulsively for being-unto-self, then his story may well turn into a fiction system that is by definition supremely unto itself" (p. 117).

5. William Stowe, *Balzac, James, and the Realistic Novel* (Princeton, N.J.: Princeton University Press, 1983), p. 40.

6. James W. Tuttleton, *The Novel of Manners in America* (New York: Norton, 1974), p. 69.

7. *The American,* p. 300. In his letters written from Paris between 1875 and 1876, James mentions frequently his own habits of reading several papers to keep abreast of French social and political life. In his letter to his father of December 22, 1875, James writes: "I find the political situation here very interesting and devour the newspapers.

The great matter for the last fortnight has been the election of seventy-five life-members of the new Senate, by the Assembly, in which the coalition of the Republicans, Legitimists and Bonapartists (which the attitude of the Orleanists has made necessary) had entirely routed the latter. The Left has carried the whole thing through with great skill and good sense, and there is a prospect of there being a very well composed Senate." *Henry James: Letters,* ed. Leon Edel, (Cambridge, Mass.: Harvard University Press, 1975), Vol. 2, p. 15.

8. John V. Antush, "The 'Much Finer Complexity' of History in *The American,*" *Journal of American Studies* 6 (April 1972):88, discusses the sixteenth- and seventeenth-century French history in *The American* primarily in terms of the beginnings of a strong bourgeoisie that would replace the aristocracy: "Since the end of the sixteenth century, when the king of France began selling small parcels of his authority to the highest bidder, the bourgeoisie, who alone held the purse strings for the economy of the nation, began to replace the aristocracy in key positions of power." Antush's rather broad view of French history causes him to treat nineteenth-century aristocratic political interests as relatively insignificant, thus reinforcing his interpretation of the Bellegardes – and Valentin in particular – as emblems of an anachronistic class: "However, the restoration of the Bourbon family to the throne of France in 1814 brought back only symbols and effected no serious change in the new political system." Nevertheless, Antush's essay deserves special mention as one of the few studies of *The American* to attempt to discuss in any detail the concrete historical details in the text. Like *The Aspern Papers* and many of James's other works, *The American* is full of such details, but the reader's surrender to the protagonist's perspective tempts us to repeat Newman's historical ignorance. James seems to take special pleasure in burying those concrete details that qualify drastically the mere impressionism of his central characters.

9. I am indebted to Professor Thomas Kavanagh of the Department of French at the University of Colorado, Boulder, for this observation.

10. Edel, ed., *Henry James: Letters,* Vol. 2, p. 30.

11. Edgar Holt, *Risorgimento: The Making of Italy, 1815–1870* (London: Macmillan, 1970), pp. 248–9. Holt describes the battle of Castelfidardo in the following terms: "The papal mercenaries fought well so long as they were facing the Italians on more or less equal terms; but as soon as Cialdini was able to deploy his whole army corps the issue was decided. . . . On the papal side 88 men were killed, 400 wounded and 600 taken prisoner. Castelfidardo was not a great victo-

ry. It was not comparable with Garibaldi's successes. But it gave the new army some useful prestige" (pp. 249–50).

12. Leon Edel and Ilse Dusoir Lind's "Introduction" to Henry James, *Parisian Sketches: Letters to the New York Tribune 1875–1876*, ed. Leon Edel and Ilse Dusoir Lind (New York: Crowell-Collier, 1961), p. 12. Further references to this work in the text are designated *PS*.

13. As early a work as it is in James's career, *The American* remains the most carefully structured in terms of what we might term the "repetition-compulsion of revenge." The loss of any viable sense of historical reality by Newman might be explained as a consequence of his entrapment in the closed circle of this revenge cycle. Newman's ostensible efforts to hold himself aloof from the chances of gaining revenge in New York and Paris in no way liberate him from the cycle, because his "renunciation" depends upon denial and repression. Innocence of man's fundamental will to power/knowledge may be the ultimate ignorance for James's characters. The only way to break the revenge cycle in James is to translate the sentimental sense of personal injury into political action. Very few of James's characters follow this course, although Hyacinth Robinson's suicide – the ultimate object of revenge is, of course, oneself – illustrates negatively how James offers his characters rather specific choices: the repetition-compulsion of revenge, absolute renunciation that merely directs enmity inward at its original source, or political action that would turn blind repetition in the direction of conscious historical change. On the psychology of revenge in James's fiction, see Mackenzie, *Communities of Honor and Love*, pp. 94–126.

14. Tuttleton writes in "A Note on the Text," in the Norton Critical Edition of *The American*, p. 315: "Whatever one may think of James's revisions for the 'New York Edition,' it is clear that the 1907 edition of *The American* is so extensively revised that it is a substantially different book from the novel James composed in the mid-1870s. In reissuing the novel, the editor must therefore choose which of the versions – early or late – should be presented."

15. R. W. Butterfield, "*The American*," in *The Air of Reality: New Essays on Henry James*, ed. John Goode (London: Methuen, 1972), pp. 9–10.

16. There is a great deal of what appears at first to be rather conventional, even heavy-handed, foreshadowing in *The American*. When reconsidered in terms of James's knowledge of the great European political events that were about to descend upon the characters in *The American*, however, this foreshadowing would be better defined as rhetorical prolepsis. We associate foreshadowing with suspense and plot,

whereas prolepsis effects a certain equation between present and future. The duel between Valentin and the German, Kapp, certainly plays upon the popular understanding of the Franco-Prussian War as a useless war fought over airy honor. Bismarck's infamous use of the Ems Dispatch to whip up German patriotism and indignation over the behavior of the French ambassadors also relied on his understanding of French national honor. Nevertheless, James's connection of the duel and the Franco-Prussian War is intended less to trivialize the war (there were very real political and territorial stakes involved) than to give some legitimacy to Valentin's absurd gesture. Looking back from the vantage point of 1875, James as much as says that Valentin's commitment to his social codes at least allows him to identify with some exactness his real enemies. In this regard, he has the advantage over Newman. Antush treats the duel as many other critics have: It is just another instance of how empty rituals have replaced the military power of the European aristocracy. See Antush, "The 'Much Finer Complexity,'" pp. 87–8.

17. *The American,* p. 306. When Tom Tristram first meets Newman in the Louvre, he asks: "What are you up to, any way? . . . Are you going to write a book?" (33). As the romantic melodrama usurps the realism of the early chapters, James has Newman increasingly figure his situation with metaphors of the popular romance, the arts, and other stylized representational modes.

4

Gender and Value in *The American*

CAROLYN PORTER

1

READERS of *The American* have always found fault with a plot resolution that leaves Christopher Newman unmarried and Claire de Cintré in a convent. Of course, readers of Henry James have always had to accommodate themselves to endings marked by renunciation. As a colleague of mine once put it, "I have never read a James novel that I did not want to hurl across the room when I finished." But *The American* presents a different case from that of, say, *The Portrait of a Lady* or *The Ambassadors*, where the reader's frustration and disappointment are, so to speak, fully earned. For as James himself conceded, in the preface he wrote for the heavily revised New York Edition of 1907, the plot of *The American* is genuinely flawed.

Whereas in 1877 James had defended *The American*'s realism, roundly denouncing those who demanded a "prettier ending" as people "who don't really know the world and who don't measure the merit of a novel by its correspondence to the same,"[1] in 1907 he frankly confesses that the novel's plot is an "affront to verisimilitude."[2] The Bellegardes "would positively have jumped," he remarks, at the opportunity to "haul" Newman and "his fortune into their boat" (*AN*, 36). Since the novel cannot be defended as realistic, James proceeds to treat it as a romance. He thus seizes the opportunity of having erred as a young realist to deliver a definition of the romance that has become a critical chestnut. "The balloon of experience is in fact of course tied to the earth," James says, and "the art of the romancer is, 'for the fun of it', insidiously to cut the cable, to cut it without our detecting him" (*AN*, 33–4).

99

James's strategy in the preface to *The American* turns out to be an instance of the romancer's art it serves to define, for by shifting his ground from the question of why he so seriously misprised the behavior of the Parisian aristocracy to the question of his faulty "invention" as a romancer, James succeeds in cutting the cable between the given case – the novel's flawed realism – and the case he transforms it into – an imperfectly executed romance.

Here, as throughout the prefaces, James treats the novel before him as a stimulus to critical meditation, and the cumulative effect of this technique is so powerful that, ever since R. P. Blackmur placed the prefaces in one volume, entitled *The Art of the Novel*, their local relevance as prefaces has justifiably taken second place to their manifold richness as a compendium of Jamesian critical theory. Yet the preface to *The American* is worth our attention *as a* preface because of the extent to which it both represses and reveals the actual sources of the novel's unsatisfactory resolution.

It is not, as James makes clear, merely a question of his having failed to "really know the world." That he had seriously misrepresented the "real note of policy in forlorn aristocracies" he openly and repeatedly admits (*AN*, 36). The more pressing question is why he had allowed himself to be so misled. In identifying the culprit as his infatuation with his "idea," James does not for a moment abandon that idea as itself worthwhile. Rather, he enables himself to defend it as the seed of a romance.

The "idea" of which he was "more than commonly enamoured" was that Christopher Newman, as representative American, should be "beguiled and betrayed," and in particular, "that he should suffer at the hands of persons pretending to represent the highest possible civilization" (*AN*, 21, 22). What gives this idea its attraction is that Newman, once "cruelly wronged," should rise above the revenge he has it in his power to inflict (*AN*, 22). This "point was of the essence," James notes, for by proving his "magnanimity," Newman would prove to be the moral superior of the Bellegardes, exposing as false their pretension "to represent the highest civilization" (*AN*, 22). In short, the charm of James's idea lies in its constitutive irony – that it is finally the Bellegardes, not Newman, who will prove commercial.

James's ardent devotion to this idea in the preface is not, like a good deal else we find there, a retrospective enthusiasm. In a letter he wrote to William Dean Howells in 1876, James describes the idea in the same terms: "My subject was: an American letting the insolent foreigner go, out of his good nature, after the insolent foreigner had wronged him and he had held him in his power. To show the good nature I must show the wrong and the wrong of course is that the American is cheated out of Mme de Cintré."[3] In the preface, James not only remains faithful to the subject's inherent charm but waxes lyrical over his "sad envy at the free play of so much unchallenged instinct," the "ecstasy of . . . ignorance" that had allowed him to imagine that he was "acutely observing – and with a blest absence of wonder at its being so easy" (*AN*, 25, 26).

Thus is the cable to the question of realism cut and the question of romance set afloat. The young author of 1876 had erred in his social observation but was, after all, "lucky to have sacrificed on this particular altar," since without his ignorance, he asks himself how he "could have written *The American*" at all (*AN*, 26). For what led him astray was his devotion to his idea, which is precisely what he now alleges made the novel a romance. He had "buried [his] head in the sand and there found beatitude" (*AN*, 21).

Yet defending *The American* as a romance proves difficult, especially given the exacting demands with which James invests that genre. Nowhere is this clearer than when he resorts to arguing that Christopher Newman was conceived as a center of consciousness. Seized by this "beautiful infatuation," James insists that it is Newman's "vision, *his* conception, *his* interpretation" that provides the novel with its coherence (*AN*, 37). Having diagnosed *The American*'s flawed realism as the result of one infatuation, with his idea, James now defends it as romance by appealing to another. But James knows better than this. As a center of consciousness, Christopher Newman is a child compared to the Isabel Archer of *The Portrait of a Lady*. Compared to Lambert Strether in *The Ambassadors*, Newman is a neonate. James grudgingly admits that he was "perhaps wrong" in thinking Newman up to the task, but finally rests his case on Newman's "more or less convincing image" (*AN*,

39). The palpable insecurity of this conclusion is reflected in the image that James leaves us of himself "clinging to [his] hero as to a tall, protective, good-natured elder brother in a rough place" (*AN*, 39).

In fact, James remains as unsatisfied with his defense of *The American* as the reader is with the novel's resolution. He confesses to being "stupified" still, since if Newman is the "lighted figure," the center of consciousness, why should he be left "severely alone" during the interval following Claire de Cintré's acceptance (AN, 38, 37, 38)? James's answer to this question is telling. What should have filled this interval was a picture of Newman and his "intended" "beautifully together," but James could not provide this picture, given the "crushing complication" he confronted: "since Madame de Cintré was after all to 'back out' every touch in the picture of her apparent loyalty would add to her eventual shame" (*AN*, 38). If Newman is to be "cruelly wronged" – and this is what provides the very opportunity for his demonstration of moral worth – the efficient agent of this cruelty must perforce be Claire de Cintré (*AN*, 22). Yet she must remain a morally beatific creature if Newman's final loss of her is to have moral weight. Little wonder that she recedes from view at the crucial moment. The fact is, she has never been very fully on view. Thus, when James adds that "with this lady, altogether, I recognize a light plank, too light a plank, is laid for the reader over a dark 'psychological' abyss," it is hard to resist the conclusion that he is doing the same thing again, laying a "light plank" at the end of the preface over a far deeper abyss in the novel than he can afford to acknowledge (*AN*, 39).

Claire de Cintré's mystification as a character is so blatant a cover-up that it compels us to press further the question of what lies behind the veil. For if there is a gap in the novel's representation of Claire de Cintré, a failure, as James puts it, to deliver the "delicate clue" to her "conduct," it is not because of a "psychological" abyss in her character (*AN*, 39). After all, her character has hardly achieved sufficient development to harbor an abyss. Rather, it is because of the role she is assigned by both James and Newman, as the embodied form of pure, transcendent value. Her emblematic status must be protected so feverishly precisely because the order of value she represents in the novel's thematic structure has threatened to disappear altogether. She is reified as a symbol in proportion to the erosion of what she symbolizes – a noncommercial, uncontaminated, and incorruptible value.

The female object of desire had figured centrally in the English novel from Richardson's day to James's without generating this particular problem. Why, then, does it erupt here? We can begin to answer this question by focusing on James's idea, whose development requires that Claire de Cintré remain beyond Newman's reach. Claire de Cintré's underdeveloped status as a character serves as a light plank over an abyss that is inevitable, given James's germinal idea, that idea to whose charm he has remained so devoted, first and last.

To understand why this is true, we need to note an odd lapse in James's accounts of *The American,* both early and late. The *proof* of Christopher Newman's moral superiority depends upon his being "wronged," as James insists in both 1876 and 1907, but what he fails to acknowledge is that Newman's *claim* to a moral destiny originates with his repudiation of money getting, the event that initiates his entire adventure. The novel is quite clear on this analogy, even if its author seems to have ignored its implications. The disgust with which Newman throws over his desire to get revenge on Wall Street at the novel's outset is loudly echoed in the disgust with which he lets the Bellegardes go at the end. This early and initiating claim to a noncommercial set of aspirations on Newman's part is significant, since it points up the fact that Newman's desire to marry Claire de Cintré is founded on his wish to enter a realm of value that transcends the one he has so dramatically exited.

As he explains to Claire, "You think of me as a fellow who has had no idea in life but to make money and drive sharp bargains. That's a fair description of me, but it's not the whole story. A man ought to care for something else, though I don't know exactly what."[4] The humor of Newman's self-confessed ignorance as to what that "something else" should be is underwritten by a certain pathos that gives his plea force. Newman's fundamental claim to our sympathy lies in his genuine desire to spring free of his commercial history, to care for "something else" (218). But of course he does not always, or even often, speak in these terms. When he discusses the wife he desires with Mrs. Tristram, he describes his ideal as "the best article in the market" (44). Newman's abandoned career as money maker, in short, has only given way to a second, as money spender, and his quest for a wife is necessarily fueled by his millions.

Consequently, his desire is unfulfillable. For the transcendent value he seeks to possess is by definition untranslatable into money. In seeking to marry Claire de Cintré, Newman wishes to acquire the unacquirable. If he were to succeed, she would have become acquirable. She would be translated into a money value, and thus would no longer possess transcendent value. Further, if this happened, the postulated basis for Newman's moral superiority — his aspiration to care for "something else" — would have vanished.

The reason for the novel's palpably forced ending, then, is that James was more devoted to sustaining a moral order of value than to anything else. His investment in his idea depended upon its adumbration of such value, and, willy-nilly, he forced his plot to confirm that value's existence. If the ending he refused would have exposed a world in which all value has been reduced to exchange value, the ending he imposed proves Newman's moral stature by enabling him to reenact that same refusal. For if Newman exposed the Bellegardes' secret to the world, he would in effect be blurting out the very discovery his dream of value forces him to repress — that there is no value except cash value, even at the heart of the "highest civilization."

A similar economy informs the preface, where James takes such pains to redeem the concept of value originally invested in his idea. By defining that idea as essentially, "charmingly — romantic," James's preface struggles to force The American into the mold of the romance, and thereby reenacts the struggle conducted in the novel, where James had to force social reality into the mold of his idea (AN, 25). His resort to treating Christopher Newman as a center of consciousness in the preface is not unlike his resort to gothic melodrama at the end of the novel; both resolutions are highly improbable and both serve the same purpose – the preservation of what James will call in a later preface "hard latent *value*" (*AN*, 120). The James of the prefaces has come to regard such value as dependent upon the imagination, the "beautiful circuit and subterfuge of our thought and our desire" to whose representation he commits the romance as a genre (*AN*, 32). But what had driven James finally to ground moral value in the artist's imagination is already apparent in *The American,* where the social ground of such value threatens to disappear.

That threat arises, ironically, because of the extent to which social reality *is* represented perceptively in *The American.* Madame de Bellegarde's commercial "audacity" is fully documented, only to be covered up by the claim, as Mrs. Tristram puts it, that the Bellegardes are "really aristocratic" and have "given [Newman] up for an idea" (152, 221). In 1876, James had believed that moral value of some sort inhered in the class distinctions of European aristocracy. As he told Howells at the time, "We are each the product of circumstances and there are stone walls which fatally divide us. I have written my story from Newman's side of the wall, and I understand so well how Mme de Cintré couldn't scramble over from her side!" This sums up the case being made by the young realist, who has argued "very materially" that if they married, Newman and Claire would have had no place to live. She couldn't have lived in New York, James insists, and once married to Newman, she couldn't have remained in France, so declassé would her marriage make her.[5] James's insistence upon the "stone walls" dividing Claire and Newman is perfectly sincere, but the novel itself portrays a society in which the walls are crumbling, eroded by the force of money.

In short, James was more of a realist than he credits himself with being in the preface, and that was the problem. For he had to thwart, throughout the novel, the force of a social observation whose representation reveals cash value swallowing moral value at every step. James's idea committed him to maintaining difference, but the novel keeps undermining it because money dissolves difference. We can now see more clearly why Claire de

Cintré is mystified as a character, for the central difference to be preserved in *The American* is not only that between America and Europe but also that between two kinds of women.

2

In "The Metropolis and Mental Life" (1903), Georg Simmel, the early-twentieth-century German sociologist, remarks, "Money is concerned only with what is common to all: it asks for the exchange value, it reduces all quality and individuality to the question: How much?"[6] Notoriously, the first word spoken by Christopher Newman in *The American*, and "the single word which constituted the strength of his French vocabulary" is "Combien?" (19). Simmel's perspective on the implications of this question acquires more pertinence when we recall the situation that provokes it. In the novel's opening scene, Newman is negotiating the purchase of a picture in the Louvre.

Much as the young James had described himself in one of his letters to the *New York Tribune*, "lounging upon an ottoman" at the exhibition of two art collections about to be sold in the Parisian "art market," Christopher Newman is introduced to us as "reclining at his ease" on a "commodious ottoman" in the Louvre, contemplating the purchase of a painting. In his *Tribune* letter, James calls attention to the difference between buying and looking when he expresses his envy at the "meditative rattle of coin in the sidepockets of amateurs not compelled, like most newspaper correspondents, to be purely platonic."[7] But his representation of Newman buying a picture in the Louvre blurs that distinction. The difference between looking and purchasing will be invoked humorously in the next chapter, where Tristram responds to Newman's announcement that he has "bought a picture" with the question, "Do they sell them?" (27). Yet the difference between the originals and the "copies that were going forward around them" is no sooner invoked than it is questioned. (17). When Tristram remarks, "these, I suppose are originals," Newman replies, "I hope so . . . I don't want a copy of a copy" (27).

Newman's response invokes two contradictory sources of value. On the one hand, the copy derives its value from the skill with

106

which it approximates the original, but this aesthetic order of value is internally unstable, as the history of art forgery amply demonstrates. A copy that imitates the original so successfully as to displace it on the market threatens to dilute its value *as* the original. If the original is to retain its inherent primary value, the distinction between it and all copies must be preserved. It is this threat, of a bad infinite regress, to which Newman playfully alludes when he says that he does not want a "copy of a copy." But he can afford to be playful about this threat because he harbors no genuine doubt about the originals on display. When it is a question of buying paintings, at least, Newman is content with copies. Indeed, we are told that he "often admired the copy much more than the original" (17).

When we inquire into the basis for his confidence in the originals, however, the economic order of value comes forcefully into view. For on what basis is the original's authenticity to be established, especially in the eyes of a naive American collector, save that it hangs where it does, in a museum, whose functional significance is to designate the paintings on display there as *not* for sale? In short, the painting's transcendent value as an aesthetic object depends upon its being priceless, upon its being removed from circulation in the art market and placed beyond the reach of money. The difference between an original and a copy, then, may putatively depend upon aesthetic criteria and operate within an aesthetic order of value, but this order itself, with its claim to an essential value, depends upon its distinction from an economic order of value. In short, the aesthetic value of an object is designated by the sign "not for sale."

It may be easy to tell the difference between Noémie's copy and Murillo's original, especially given how bad that copy is, but the more fundamental issue raised in James's presentation of the Louvre as the scene of a commercial transaction is that which is also suggested by the obvious envy of the "newspaper correspondent" at the Parisian art auction – the issue of whether there *is* a realm of value beyond the reach of Newman's millions, a realm that resists the power of money to erase the difference between original and copy, and thus to eradicate any order of value that is not, finally, commercial. This issue becomes the more pressing when the original and the copy in question are not paintings, but women.

Although he is at first comically obtuse to just what is being offered for sale by Noémie Nioche, Christopher Newman himself shifts the focus from paintings to women when he shifts his attention not merely from pictures to copies but from copy to copyist. Again, Simmel provides the keynote for understanding what renders difficult James's effort to mark the difference between a transcendent value and a commercial one. In *The Philosophy of Money,* Simmel remarks that "the abhorrence that modern 'good' society entertains towards the prostitute . . . declines with the increase in the price for her services," because an "exhorbitant price saves the object for sale from the degradation that would otherwise be part of the fact of being offered for sale."[8] Noémie Nioche displays in this scene a thorough understanding of the inflationary principle Simmel describes, the principle by which sufficient money can decontaminate and finally mystify prostitution. Noémie responds to Newman's "Combien?" with a price she herself regards as exorbitant. When he asks, "for a copy, isn't that a good deal?" Newman is already revealing the desire for an original that will take the form of his pursuit of Claire de Cintré, as well as his acumen as a man of business who knows what a copy should cost as compared to the original. But Noémie is also acute, insiting that her "copy has remarkable qualities; it is worth nothing less" (20).

It is symptomatic of Noémie's relatively impoverished state that even the most preposterous sum she can bring herself to name cannot inflate the value of her painting sufficiently to impress Newman. Nor is he altogether deceived. He realizes that she "had asked too much" but "bore her no grudge for doing so," since he initially thinks her honest in her high estimate of the copy's merits and since he understands her attitude as that of a good businesswoman, bargaining for the highest price possible (26). What Newman has not yet perceived, of course, is that Noémie is actually interested in selling herself rather than her picture. Indeed, the comedy of the scene as a whole is produced by the ironic gap between Noémie's blatant flirtation and Newman's remarkable misreading of it. When Noémie deposits "a rosy blotch in the middle of the Madonna's cheek" to demonstrate her capacity to finish the painting "in perfection," Newman's exclamation, "too red, too red . . . her complexion is more delicate," reveals the extent to which James is willing to broaden the joke on his hero (20). For us, in short, there is never a question about Noémie's intentions, so that the inflationary principle invoked in her sale of the copy carries over automatically to her implicit effort to sell herself. Given her own "remarkable qualities," she will not be cheap, and she makes this even clearer when she imitates a young lady of breeding in her response to Newman's request for her card. "My father will wait upon you," she says, but as her coy imitation is lost upon Newman, she has to drive it home: "Happily for you, you are an American. It's the first time I ever gave my card to a gentleman" (21).

Noémie's entire performance in this scene signals her high ambition to join the ranks of those courtesans whose talent for copying the habits and fashions of the upper classes provoked complaints such as the following from a contemporary Parisian journalist: "Everything brings together the demi-monde and the monde entier: everything allows us to confuse things which should not even be aware of one another's existence. . . . The nobleman's wife from the Faubourg St. Germain passes, on the staircase at Worth's, the elegant female from the Quartier Breda."[9]

If Noémie is a copy of the upper-class women whose ranks she aspires to join, Claire de Cintré is the original *par excellence*. The scene in which Newman appears before Madame de Bellegarde to offer his suit for Claire echoes the opening scene, although now the commercial offer is made in the sanctified space not of the Louvre, but of the Faubourg. Newman appeared to Noémie as a potential client, a man who might provide financial support for her rise into society in exchange for her sexual services. Now he appears to Madame de Bellegarde as a potential financial resource, one whose fortune might be large enough to buy her daughter's hand in marriage. Her response, "How rich?" echoes his opening "Combien?" Like Newman at the Louvre, Madame de Bellegarde is in the position of power here, despite the fact that, like Noémie, she is the seller, not the buyer. But then hers is a seller's market. Unlike Noémie or her copy, what Madame de Bellegarde has to sell is theoretically of inordinate value. Claire de Cintré is an original, so that the only question here is whether Newman has sufficient millions to buy the social equivalent of the "Mona Lisa."

Despite the apparent contrast between Noémie and Claire, the copy and the original, what is to keep us from seeing in Madame de Bellegarde's performance the same inflationary principle we saw at work in Noémie's bargaining with Newman? That is, is not Madame de Bellegarde exacting an exorbitant price in order to mystify and thereby deny Claire's degradation as an object for sale? There is, after all, no question that Madame de Bellegarde wishes to sell her daughter in marriage. She has already done it once, and been cheated of the fortune she expected in return. Given the lengths to which she has gone the first time, it is hardly surprising that she is even more wary and calculating than before. In allowing Newman's suit to go forward while not approving of him, she presumably intends to keep other options in view. What she does not, however, apparently bargain for is that her precious possession will retreat to a convent and thus preserve her status as undegradable, as without a price.

Madame de Bellegarde has already, however, proven a faulty judge of her daughter. From the moment Newman arrives on the scene, Claire's behavior begins to startle her. When Claire appears dressed for a ball on the same evening that Newman has come to meet her mother, the latter declares her daughter "strange" and "audacious," and wonders aloud "what has taken possession of my daughter?" (126–7). In deciding to marry Newman, Claire again amazes her mother, who doubtless has assumed that her daughter's fine breeding would preclude his success. But Claire apparently sees in Newman the possibility of eluding the marketplace in which her mother wants to place her. Although the clues to Claire's conduct are indeed delicate, they do suggest that her attraction to Newman begins at the moment he claims that "you ought to be perfectly free, and marriage will make you so" (115). In response to this promise, Claire moves "toward . . . Newman" with "the air of a woman who had stepped across the frontier of friendship and, looking round her, finds the regions vast" (115). If Newman's proposal appears to Claire a means of escaping her marketable status, her mother's blocking of that escape leaves her little choice. In finally defying her mother, that is,

Claire refuses to be "sold again," as Mrs. Tristram puts it, but the extreme to which Claire is driven in the effort to escape the marketplace reveals the extent to which the assertion of transcendent value is threatened by the commercial values that dominate Parisian society (79).

Further, it marks the extreme to which James himself was driven in his effort to forge and sustain the distinction between commercial and transcendent values. Like the originals in the Louvre, to remain not for sale Claire must be entombed behind the convent's high walls and iron railings. The price of being priceless is a living death, a state in which Claire is hardly in a position to embody anything. For what differentiates the museum from the convent as the last refuge of undegradable and transcendent value is that the museum at least displays its treasures, whereas the convent hides its members from view. Perhaps this is necessary, since after all the museum has proven vulnerable, in the opening scene, to the invasion of commerce. Since all evidence of the Carmelites' physical existence is reduced to the mere sound of their voices, they are presumably safe.

The gothic extremity of this plot resolution testifies to the improbable lengths to which James was driven in *The American* by the need to affirm a locus of value untainted by money. Further, it sets in relief the question that plot resolution serves to beg. Put most directly, that question is, on what ground can we distinguish two women who are for sale, except by the difference in their price?

On the one hand, plot and counterplot are designed to establish and develop the difference between commercial and transcendent value on the conventional basis of that between bad and good women. On the other hand, the two plots threaten to converge. Indeed, had James suffered the marriage between Newman and Claire to take place, that threat would come close to being realized, on precisely the ground he takes, and inflicts such narrative pains to avoid — that of a common, commercially determined value. For not only would this marriage signify that Claire *had* a price, specifically the unreported sum that Newman names to Madame de Bellegarde, but further, it would be curiously mirrored in the final alliance between Noémie and Lord Deepmere. If both women were

111

sold, that is, the only difference between them would be their price, and even that distinction would have begun to fade, since Noémie approaches Claire's social height by raising her price to a level commensurate with that at which Claire's mother has been willing to sell her daughter.

As it is, Noémie's social rise follows from and depends upon her moral fall, but the former is so spectacular that the latter hardly matters. As Lord Deepmere explains to Newman in Hyde Park, as regards Noémie's role in Valentin's demise, "she couldn't help it, you know, and Bellegarde was only my twentieth cousin," and anyway, "she isn't known yet, and she's in such very good form" (300). Noémie does not, of course, actually rise to join the ranks of the nobility; we do not expect Lord Deepmere to marry her. But she does rise to float above class distinctions, and thereby to blur them, a dénouement that is far more disturbing than her marriage to Lord Deepmere would be. For as the Parisian journalist previously quoted reveals, it is the confusion of "things which should not even be aware of one another's existence" that produces anxiety. Noémie Nioche proves far better at copying the nobility's style and manner than she is at copying Murillo.

If, at the novel's end, she has joined Lord Deepmere and thus blurred class lines on the surface of the plot, her role in bringing about Valentin's death has blurred them at a deeper level. Noémie has not, of course, actually murdered Valentin, but then he would certainly be alive had he not become interested in her. By the same token, Madame de Bellegarde has not exactly murdered her husband, but then it is clear that had she not intervened in his medical care, he would have survived his illness. In short, if not murder, then, say, manslaughter lies behind both Noémie's rise in value on the market and Madame de Bellegarde's first sale of her daughter.

The two stories do not converge, thanks to James's strenuous efforts, but the class lines dividing the two women are obscured. Further, the major moral distinction between them – that Claire refuses to be "sold again," whereas Noémie sells herself again and again – itself begins to fade in the light of the common social condition that the novel suggests has led to both women's commodification – the decay of a patriarchal authority and protection.

3

The paternal authority of both M. Nioche and the murdered marquis has been overturned by their wives. Their daughters are thus left to fend for themselves in a social world where their fate as individuals depends upon the exchange value they can command. In Noémie's case, the lack of paternal authority is foregrounded; in Claire's, it is the lack of paternal protection. But authority and protection are fundamentally related by their dependence upon a paternal power that is absent in both cases.

When Newman asks M. Nioche whether his daughter obeys him, the latter retorts, "She can't obey, monsieur, since I don't command" (57). Married to a "bad woman" now "gone to her account," M. Nioche has undergone financial reverses that have left him a "reduced capitalist" (55). In his memory, the occasion on which he "found" his wife "out" coincides with the beginning of his financial decline (24). His "miseries" arrived in the dual form of his "dark days" and his "explosion with Madame Nioche" (57). It is therefore unclear to what extent M. Nioche's paternal impotence results from being cuckolded and to what extent from losing his money. But that he is powerless to control his daughter is clear. As he abjectly confesses, "she is stronger than I" (57). In Newman's eyes, at least, it is M. Nioche's impotence that enables Noémie to become a "little adventuress," placing herself on the market, where she proves, as Valentin recognizes, "a great one" (134).

One proof of Noémie's genius is that she turns her relationship with her father into a parody of paternal protection. He comes to fetch her each day from the Louvre and acts his own "high-toned" part in the play, but she is directing it, as Valentin sees instantly. But then he is interested in Noémie. Newman's "interest," in contrast, lies in her father (64). When Valentin bets him that M. Nioche will not prove a Virginius, Newman takes the bet, saying, "if the old man turns out a humbug, you may do what you please. I wash my hands of the matter" (136). M. Nioche does turn out a humbug, but Newman cannot altogether wash his hands of the matter, since Valentin's pursuit of Noémie turns out to place him in jeopardy. Newman's loyalty thus shifts from M. Nioche to his friend Valentin, both of whom need protection from Noémie. As Valentin tells Newman, "For the girl herself, you may be at rest. I don't know what harm she may do to me, but I certainly can't hurt her" (136). Given M. Nioche's lack of paternal power, Noémie is loosed upon the market, where it is men who need protection from her. It is worth keeping in mind that Newman proves no more capable of protecting Valentin from her than he has of protecting M. Nioche.

In the case of Madame de Cintré, the cause of paternal impotence is somewhat clearer. Not only is her father dead, but he was hastened to his grave precisely because he had prohibited his wife's sale of his daughter in marriage. Again, as in the story of M. Nioche's decline, money is identified with women, but here the relation is direct and causal. Madame de Bellegarde usurps the power of the father in order to transform her daughter into a commodity whose sale will replenish the family coffers. Left without her father's protection and obliged to obey a mercenary mother, Claire falls into the flow of exchange value. Valentin cannot save her from this fate, and Urbain is complicit in forcing it upon her. With the death of the father, the family is corrupted from within by the ambition of the mother.

Once freed by widowhood from this victimization, Claire tries to protect herself by striking a bargain with her mother, whose every command she agrees to obey save one, the command to marry again. Thus does she hope to preserve her rewon status as not for sale. But without paternal protection, she remains vulnerable. From her first appearance in the novel, if we credit Mrs. Tristram's interpretations, Claire is being harassed by her mother, who apparently regards her bargain with her daughter in the same light that she regards her word of honor to Newman — as a strategy, not a promise. In any case, Claire's continued vulnerability results less from her mother's dishonesty than from the pecuniary interest it serves. For what renders Claire's exemption from commodity status fragile is that she is too valuable *not* to be sold. Up to a point, Claire's very expensiveness serves to protect her; her mother's ambition, after all, is of a high order, and there are few men with sufficient millions even to make a bid. But when Newman proves able to meet her price and Claire consents to marry him, Madame de Bellegarde presumably considers all promises suspended and the auction again open. In the absence of her father's power to protect her, Claire is left in the same position that Noémie occupies; she must "be converted into specie" or face up to "burying herself alive" (53).

Gerda Lerner has recently argued that one of the earliest forms in which two classes of women were distinguished is expressed in Middle Assyrian Law 40, which designates who can and cannot be veiled. As Lerner decodes the law, it reveals that respectable women are those "protected by their men," whereas unrespectable women are those left "unprotected."[10] Although Lerner's interest in this law leads her analysis in a somewhat different direction, and although the society the law served is quite alien to nineteenth-century Paris, I think the distinction she identifies can shed light on James's diagnosis of Parisian society as the scene of paternal powerlessness. For that scene reveals a world in which a patriarchal nobility has been undermined by the corrosive force of capitalism. No doubt the aging marquis had been a rake, but what killed him was not his sins but his wife's greed. Valentin is also a bit of a rake, but a fine fellow nevertheless, and what kills him is, effectively, Noémie's greed. The duel he fights over her, as she puts it, "will make her fortune" (207). Noémie and Madame de Bellegarde are sellers on the market, and Claire is sold there, but all have been reduced to functions of the cash nexus, and by the same forces that have already undermined paternal power.

A major social transformation from patriarchy to capitalism has taken place beneath the surface of Parisian society as James represents it, and its consequences are most vividly expressed in the threat that transformation poses to the traditional distinction between two classes of women. When fathers command authority, they can both control and protect their daughters. Under these conditions, it is possible to mark off respectable from unrespectable women, since the former *are* protected. But as traditional patriarchal power is displaced by the commercial power of the marketplace, this distinction breaks down. Women cannot be protected, but neither can they be controlled. Even the ethereal Claire repudiates her mother's authority in the end. Most significantly with respect to James's problems as a novelist, under these transformed conditions the two classes of women cannot be distinguished. It is testimony to the central role of women as the decisive form of all value in this scenario that when this distinction breaks down, the very concept of value is thrown into doubt.

At the highest level of abstraction, of course, women have always been forms of exchange value.[11] James's novel is not written at that level, of course. Rather, he has simply appropriated a set of novelistic conventions, traceable to *Clarissa* on the one hand and to *Moll Flanders* on the other, and put them into play in accord with his plot demands, but these demands force him to the edge of an abyss. In sum, when patriarchy breaks down, and with it the distinction between women under and not under male control and protection, all women are left unprotected and uncontrolled. The only distinction remaining is that between those who are for sale and those who are not, and this difference in turn begins to blur.

Thus, I propose, did James dig a hole in his path. His need to portray Newman as cruelly wronged led him to see more deeply into the corruption of French society than his idea had led him to expect. Having made his hero's moral status dependent upon his adherence to a moral value traditionally vested in women, he found himself forced to cover up the vacuum left by the absence of such value.

Accordingly, in the novel James is compelled to erect a set of defenses against the progressively unfolding revelation of an absence of value. Valentin's demonstrated honor as an ally of Newman to the bitter end is the most powerful of these defenses, since Valentin is the sole male member of the Bellegarde family who embodies a genuine moral imagination. Yet once beguiled by the charms of Noémie, Valentin is doomed by the very principles of honor that have elevated him above his family. As a stay against the confusion of values displayed around him, Valentin lacks force, to say the least. As both he and Claire point out to Newman, Valentin has nothing to do. Regarded by his elder brother and his mother as the black sheep of the family, he is in fact the last, along with Claire, of what Newman sees as the fine and noble strain in the family bloodline. His death testifies to the hollowness of his concept of honor in a world that can provide no place for its survival. Yet, like his sister, Valentin does at least function as a symbol of the moral value that ought to inhere in the "highest civilization," and his friendship with Newman helps to authenticate the latter's aspiration to believe in something besides money getting.

Another defense James develops against the erosion of value takes the form of lowering his sights from "honor" to "respectability." Respectability is further identified as English, rather than French, largely through its association with Mrs. Bread. As Claire's surrogate mother and Newman's surrogate partner in a rather ludicrous midnight tryst, Mrs. Bread stands in for the missing lover and refers us to a solid English culture for evidence of the familial loyalties missing in Paris.[12] As her name all too blatantly suggests, she is an arbitrary symbol of solid and unpretentious virtue.

The chief indicator of both of these characters' virtue, however, is their admiration for Newman, whose moral stature itself must provide the keystone for the arch James builds to cover the gap his novel has exposed. Seen, as the preface suggests James finally regarded him, as the ultimate defense against the disappearance of authentic value, Newman requires closer scrutiny.

4

We can begin to observe what is most curious about Newman's behavior as moral exemplar by comparing his response to Madame de Bellegarde's mistreatment of him with Valentin's response to Stanislas Kapp's "offence" (209). The two scenes follow each other in chapters 17 and 18. No doubt we heartily agree with Newman's judgment that Valentin is "too good to go and get [his] throat cut for a prostitute" (211–12). In trying to dissuade Valentin from this "wretched theatrical affair," Newman expresses himself in terms that epitomize American common sense and masculine force: "Because your great-grandfather was an ass, is that any reason why you should be? . . . I think I could manage him yet." Valentin replies, "you can't invent anything that will take the place of satisfaction for an insult" (211).

Although it is clear enough that Valentin's duel with the "sanguineous" son of a "rich brewer of Strasbourg" is a most pathetic "remnant" of the "high-tempered time" to which Valentin refers it, it is also clear, or rather proves so in the following chapter, that Newman *is* unable to "invent" anything to take the duel's place as "satisfaction for an insult" (211). If Valentin gets his "throat cut for a prostitute," he at least avenges his honor as a man. "A man," as he explains to Newman, "can't back down before a woman" (209). Yet Newman does just that. Confronted by Madame de Bellegarde's repudiation, he feels "sick, and suddenly helpless," and emerges from her house "too stunned and wounded for consecutive action" (219, 220). Although the major contrast established in these two chapters is that between Valentin's authentic honor and his family's lack of it, Newman's ineffective response to what is manifestly an insult as well as a betrayal conjures forth a secondary contrast between him and Valentin as masculine figures.

In both scenes, Newman protests "violently," but with utterly no effect (211). Furthermore, in the second, Newman himself calls attention to the fact that Claire's mother has "frightened her, . . . bullied her, . . . *hurt* her" (218). So he is not only backing down before one woman, he is failing to protect another. Newman's behavior here strikingly lacks the masculine force he has claimed to possess when he says to Valentin, "If a man hits you, hit him back; if a man libels you, haul him up" (211). Of course, Madame de Bellegarde is not a man, but the "authority" she invokes in her confrontation with Newman makes her as hard as the "stone" to which Newman compares Noémie when he insists to Valentin, "I don't call her a woman" (215, 209). His straightforward statement in chapter 17 about how to respond to mistreatment figures as part of Newman's healthy and direct, distinctively American, perspective. But it rings a bit false in retrospect, as Newman stands there vainly insisting to the Bellegardes, "A man can't be used in this fashion" (217). Clearly, he can be. Clearly, he has been.

Such an account of Newman's impotence may seem churlish and unfair, and in a sense it is. Newman has no choice, really, but to back down at this point, particularly in view of Claire's behavior. Yet it is precisely the fact that he has no choice, the fact that the plot dictates that he have none, that is noteworthy, since it is that which makes him impotent. If this is true, then his final repudiation of revenge is the more telling. Before turning to that subject, let me clarify the point at issue here.

If the Bellegardes mistreat Newman, he could readily protest that James has done the same, for Newman is not only slated for failure by his assigned task of desiring to acquire the unacquirable, he is also placed in a role that threatens to feminize him. Let me emphasize the terms "role" and "threaten," for Newman is virtually the only vigorous and robust male hero James was ever to create in a novel, a notable fact that might be explained on psychological and biographical grounds. But I am not concerned here with the nest of questions surrounding James's own sexual anxieties, rich and provocative as these have become in recent years.[13] In other words, I am concerned not with James's expressed or repressed attitudes toward sex, but with his representational use of gender. From this point of view, Newman's exceptional status as an unequivocally masculine hero may be seen as the kind of exception that proves a rule, the rule that is instituted in *The Portrait of a Lady*. For what led James to transform his innocent American into what he promised Howells would be a "female Newman"[14] can be inferred from examining the extent to which Newman's role in *The American* — his role as distinguished from the virtually innate masculinity with which James tries to invest him as a character — threatens to feminize him.

If we return now to the issue of Newman's final revenge, we can first observe that he more than makes up for his pathetic retreat in chapter 18. He confronts Madame de Bellegarde and her son Urbain together in the Parc Monceau and, "tingling . . . with passion," thoroughly enjoys presenting them with his evidence and torturing them with the threat of exposure (281). As if this were not enough, he is visited the next day by the ever diligent Urbain, who has summoned up in the interim more ingenuity than he had displayed the previous day in claiming that Newman's evidence is a forgery. At the close of this second interview, Newman exclaims, "Well, I ought to be satisfied now!" (288). But such satisfaction as he has gained turns to disgust when he tries to make good on his threats. Calling upon the "comical duchess," he is suddenly faced with "the folly of his errand," having "morally . . . turned a sort of somersault" (289, 291). His satisfaction, when it finally arrives, is the "strange satisfaction" that descends on him later as he stands outside of the "dumb, deaf, inanimate" walls of Claire's living tomb on the rue d'Enfer and gives her up as lost forever (305).

Thus is the necessary resolution imposed and Newman redeemed as a moral hero, but in terms that undermine his masculinity. That James feels the pressure exerted by this problem is clear from the amount of conventional satisfaction he affords Newman before he is forced into his moral somersault. In the scene in the park, Newman enjoys "all the vengeance" he wants, as he later tells Mrs. Tristram, since he is sure he has provoked fear in Madame de Bellegarde (309). Her remarkable courage in the face of such fear even provokes his respect: "You're a mighty plucky woman," he tells her. "It's a great pity you have made me your enemy. I should have been one of your greatest admirers" (285). In effect, Newman has fought a duel here and come away with his honor intact. It is only after Urbain visits him the next day that Newman's satisfaction starts to disintegrate, as James lays the ground for Newman's final repudiation of his vengeful threat. In short, the scene in the park has served to reaffirm Newman's masculinity as forcefully as possible at the last moment available to James before his hero's moral ascendance is negotiated. Once Newman turns away in moral disgust and derives his "satisfaction" from accepting loss rather than avenging insult, his masculinity is again threatened, as it had been earlier when he retreated from Madame de Bellegarde's drawing room. For no matter how absurd Valentin's duel may have been, the code of honor it represents is allied with masculinity. Indeed, from the opening presentation of M. Nioche, that "exquisite image of shabby gentility," to the description of Valentin's rooms with their "faded tapestries," their "rusty arms and ancient panels and platters," their "floors muffled in the skins of beasts," the novel relentlessly associates masculinity with the forms of a patriarchal past, no matter how moth-eaten and decayed it has become. Newman's own "gilded saloons on the Boulevard Haussmann," by contrast, associate him with a modern, commercially defiled world, as does his taste for garish splendor (22, 96).

120

As Newman sees it, his quest for revenge has led him "very near being an ass," a condition he has already associated with Valentin's great-grandfather and the code of honor his dueling tradition maintains. It is not clear, however, how one *avoids* being an ass *without* such traditions. As he leaves the duchess's house, Newman wonders "whether, after all, he was not an ass not to have discharged his pistol" (292). Newman knows how to use a pistol; as he has told Valentin, "I wish it were pistols. . . . I could show you how to lodge a bullet" (209). Yet James does allow Newman to discharge his pistol in the scene in the park. If, as Newman believes, "words were acts," the words he utters to Madame de Bellegarde are violent ones: "Looking her straight in the eyes," he says, "You killed your husband" (281–2). Nevertheless, as the closing scene of the novel reveals, it is by no means clear that Newman has lodged any bullets. Newman admits that the Bellegardes have not been "humbled," but he insists that "they were afraid." It is Mrs. Tristram, however, who has the final word. She explains that the Bellegardes were "probably" not frightened, after all, but bluffed Newman on the basis of their "confidence" in his "good nature." When Newman "instinctively" turns to see if his evidence has burned up, he is in effect reaching again for his pistol.

James is still trying to mediate here between the demands of his plot and the threat it poses to his hero's masculinity, and this is about the best he can do. For the plot has called from the outset for Newman's victimization. "Beguiled and betrayed," as James calls him in the preface, Newman is already situated by James's idea in the traditional role of a woman seduced and betrayed, and what makes him vulnerable is precisely that "good nature" on which Mrs. Tristram claims that the Bellegardes rely. Repeatedly invoked as his identifying trait, this good nature is what makes Newman want to observe the necessary customs, to resist quarreling with Claire's family, and to dissuade Valentin from fighting the duel. When Claire tells him, "you are too good-natured," she passed judgment on his refusal to respond with any apparent vigor to Urbain's dislike of him (159). Perhaps this is one of those "delicate clues" to Claire's conduct, for here she seems actually to want Newman to fight for her.

121

Newman's good nature is most crudely exploited by the young marquise when she proposes that he take her into the demimonde. As she puts it, "All I ask of you is to give me your arm; you are less compromising than anyone else. I don't know why, but you are" (202). What makes Newman "less compromising than anyone else" is presumably his status as an American who stands outside the world of class gradations that Urbain's wife finds so restricting. Yet her proposition, by taking advantage of Newman's detached social position, has the effect of transforming it into that of the courtesan, whose ability to float above class distinctions and to move freely across all social boundaries is exemplified by Noémie Nioche. Of course, Noémie and the young marquise are themselves mirror images of one another. The marquise "reminded Newman of his friend, Mademoiselle Nioche; this was what that much-obstructed young lady would have liked to be" (121). If Noémie floats across class boundaries by emulating the model embodied in the marquise, the latter young woman would like to enjoy a similar freedom. Their aspirations converge. Yet this convergence cannot entirely obscure another, between Noémie and Newman, which the marquise's proposal suggests. She wishes to enjoy social freedom without "undue risk" to her reputation, but in propositioning Newman, she is not only indifferent to his but eager to exploit its lack of definition. Newman's agreement to oblige her only after his marriage serves to underscore the impropriety implicit in her request. When the planned marriage falls through, the marquise resorts to another outsider, Lord Deepmere, whose respect for propriety in any case is rather less acute than Newman's.

Newman's good nature operates as a signifier of his Americanness, but it also turns out to signify an incipiently female vulnerability. Once we begin to observe such contradictions at the center of his character, they become manifest at the representational surface of the novel as well. For example, when James introduces Newman as "a powerful specimen of an American," he associates the fact that "he never smoked" with an American image of "health and strength" (18). It is not because Newman is careful to preserve such health that he does not smoke. On the contrary, "he had been assured . . . that cigars were excellent for the health" and was "quite capable of believing it," but his health, as James is taking pains to point out, is of that inherently robust kind "which the owner does nothing to 'keep up'." As a representative American, Newman is unreflective and un-self-conscious, traits that poor Mr. Babcock finds quite distressing. Newman is in fact too much the robust and healthy American male for Mr. Babcock, but as Newman remarks in his letter to Mrs. Tristram, he is too much the "Methodist . . . old lady" for his English traveling companion (76). Meanwhile, Newman's temperateness as a non-smoker, introduced as a mark of his American vigor, marks him off from the sexually charged male world in which Valentin and Mr. Tristram are always smoking or asking if it is allowed. Newman's gilded rooms strike Valentin as too large for smoking, whereas his own small abode is suffused with the scent of tobacco mixed with perfume. Apparently, American masculinity lacks not only force, but sexual energy as well.

The cross-signals of a threatened masculinity inscribed in such signs of Newman's Americanness register a tension built into James's treatment of his hero that is already visible in the opening description of him. Christopher Newman is seated in the Louvre, "staring at Murillo's beautiful moon-borne Madonna" after a wearying day of looking "out all the pictures to which an asterisk was affixed . . . in his Baedeker." Described as "long, lean, and muscular," Newman is carefully associated with masculine "vigour" and "toughness," traits underscored by James's remark that Newman "had often performed great physical feats which left him less jaded than his tranquil stroll through the Louvre" (17). Newman is, in short, a vigorous American male, comically afflicted with an "aesthetic headache" brought on by his atypical "exertions" as an aesthetic spectator, and yet the pose in which he comes into view for us as readers conflicts strikingly with this fact. "Reclining at his ease" on a "great circular divan," a "commodious ottoman," and in "serene possession of its softest spot," the "jaded" Newman is identified not only with "weak-kneed lovers of the fine arts" but also with what those arts themselves would have displayed as a feminine pose. A man looking at a painting of a woman, Newman is simultaneously a man posed as a woman. Indeed, one might compare his posture to that of the courtesan in Manet's "Olympia."

The vulnerability inscribed in Newman's pose is signaled by James's effort to protect him when he remarks, "We have approached him, perhaps, at a not especially favourable moment; he is by no means sitting for his portrait" (19). Yet that is precisely what Newman is doing by unwittingly obliging the "observer" James conjures forth to take his measure as American. Accordingly, James must take pains to save Newman, as male gazer and subject, from being absorbed by the pose James has placed him in, as female object of a male gaze. Thus it is stressed that Newman is persistently looking at women, whether they be pictures, copies, or copyists.

We might give many examples of other narrative sites at which Newman's masculinity is threatened, but the point I wish to make is that it cannot avoid being threatened from the moment James undertakes to develop his idea. By creating a "female Newman" in Isabel Archer, James solved not only this problem but also the more blatant one he took note of in the preface. That is, by making his American a woman, he appropriated the right gender for a protagonist doomed to victimization at the hands of a corrupt European civilization. Further, if moral value had turned up missing at the site of the novel's generic type, the female object of desire, he restored that value in a new type, the female subject of desire, and invested her with value himself, a value adumbrated by the consciousness she develops.

In order for that development to be displayed, of course, Isabel too must be "beguiled and betrayed"; her consciousness blossoms forth in the midnight vigil in chapter 42 of *The Portrait of a Lady,* where she realizes for the first time that she has been deceived. In other words, James remains committed to a moral economy of loss, but Isabel Archer's demonstration of moral superiority through loss does not threaten her gender identity. It confirms it.

Further, the moral economy of loss to which Newman's "strange satisfaction" is inadequately referred, with Isabel Archer becomes fully operational. Newman has lost Claire, but we cannot know what, exactly, that loss means, since Claire remains a virtual blank. But we know quite well what Isabel Archer has lost — her freedom. As the female subject of desire, Isabel marries an Osmond whom she regards as a kind of transcendent gentleman, a natural aristocrat with whom she will enjoy sharing a supreme freedom. But when he proves a sham, the values Isabel has mistakenly projected onto him are not thrown into doubt, nor is her dream of freedom exposed as itself without foundation. Married for her money, she has not been reduced to money, since she has been accorded an identity grounded in the "beautiful circuit and subterfuge of [her] thought and [her] desire," and her failed marriage only sets in relief what has been lost — the freedom to realize that identity in the world. In Isabel's consciousness, James finds a site on which to locate value.

5

James's creation of a "female Newman" represents only the next step in what was to become a long and perilous journey in search of narrative methods for redeeming the "hard latent value" from what he came to regard as life's "splendid waste" (*AN,* 120). To trace his course along this path would lead us on a virtually endless journey ourselves, but it is at least possible to look down that road from the vantage point of *The American,* whose flaws turn out to serve as delicate clues to James's later conduct.

If a female Newman solved many problems for James, *The Portrait of a Lady* reveals as well the price paid for these solutions. By making Isabel a subject rather than an object, he can turn to narrative advantage her social condition as object — whether of Goodwood's insistent male desire or of Madame Merle's mercenary and maternal exploitation. Since marriage serves not as a goal but as a trap in this plot, Isabel's serial evasion of that trap allows James the room to elaborate a basis for the interior freedom of consciousness that his heroine is designed to exhibit, in retrospect, once she has fallen into that trap. Yet he frees her as subject from the commodity status she possesses as object only to become, in effect, *his* subject. His aim is to redeem value, the value conventionally inscribed in woman, from a world in which it has been threatened by commodification, but James's means of saving this value markedly resembles the behavior of a patriarchal father who uses his authority both to protect and to control his daughter.

Most obviously, James's protection takes the form of openly soliciting the reader's patience on Isabel's behalf, particularly at those moments when she is in danger of being misunderstood or taken too lightly. But the power to protect is also, inevitably, the power to control, as Ralph Touchett's inability to do either readily demonstrates. Unlike Ralph, James has such power, even though he take pains to conceal it, and the form that his control takes reveals what is most in need of protection – not Isabel herself, but the value she has come to embody as a result of the freedom of imagination with which James has endowed her. The Isabel Archer whose freedom as a fictional subject James applauds when he celebrates it in the preface to the *Portrait* as the idea that germinated *this* novel, ends up as the Isabel Archer who is fixed within the portrait that the novel becomes. Since woman as the representational form of value has been turned into money by a modern economy that transforms all value into exchange value, James redeems that value from the "splendid waste" by reinscribing patriarchal power in the role of the author who protects Isabel's value by placing her in a portrait. Like Claire retreating to her convent, Isabel herself must return behind the stone walls of Osmond's dark prison, but her value remains enshrined in the portrait for which, like Newman, she has unwittingly been sitting throughout her adventure.

James not only redeems her value, he retains possession of it at the same time. Indeed, in exchange for the price of his exertions, he has in effect purchased an "original," which the preface serves to place in his own personal Louvre – the New York Edition. In short, if James's protection and control enact a patriarchal role, the power on which his authority draws can best be described by analogy with Newman's millions. For the author who assumes the role of patriarchal father must bring to bear the kind of incalculable resources of imagination on which James presents himself drawing in the prefaces, where he speaks of the artist "investing and reinvesting" his "germ, his grain of gold" in accord with a "sublime economy of art" that resembles nothing so much as the sublime economy of capital. The value of James's idea, his "germ," in other words, is not merely a value to be redeemed and saved but a value to be invested and reinvested.

The economy in question is fully exhibited in James's last completed novel, *The Golden Bowl*, where James himself effectively finishes the task he set for Newman, the transfer of value from European to American hands by the acquisition of the unacquirable. By placing Maggie Verver in Newman's role and Prince Amerigo in Claire's, James reverses the genders of his American seeker after and his European vessel of value, and thereby finally resolves the dilemma to which *The American* had introduced him. The prince is an original who is purchased, but his value is not thereby reduced to money. On the contrary, it grows in proportion to his demonstrated sexual desirability, for Charlotte Stant's desire augments his sexual attraction in Maggie's eyes. Unlike Claire, Amerigo is not a blank space, nor is he, like Osmond, a sham; his value is a given, but it must be invested and reinvested through a "beautiful circuit and subterfuge of . . . desire" in order to be expressed. Meanwhile, Maggie's desire as a female subject is distinguished from her father's acquisitive desires as collector, without her losing the force of his money. So, unlike Newman, she is not undermined from the outset by the contamination of money. She loses her father, but she gains a prince. The cost, to Charlotte in particular, of the marriage that is finally saved is high, but the marriage does finally accomplish that appropriation of the value of the "highest civilization" that Newman's adventure had failed to produce. In *The Golden Bowl*, James cashed in on two discoveries that are traceable to *The American* and its problems. He had already, in *The Portrait of a Lady*, learned that the American bearer of money had to be female, but now he found that the European bearer of value had to be male. Under these conditions, originals could enter the marketplace, which was the only place through which they could pass from a European past to an American future.

In 1876, James had written to the *New York Tribune* about a recent acquisition by an American art collector, and had expressed his own "acute satisfaction in seeing America stretch out her long arm and rake in, across the green cloth of the wide Atlantic, the highest prizes in the game of civilization."[15] By restoring the father's power in the form of Adam Verver's millions, James as a patriarchal capitalist no longer needed to envy the buyers on the Parisian art market. He could now "lay down his money with one hand and take with the other" in the "perfect security" of knowing that he was purchasing originals.[16] For what James had wanted all along was what Newman had aspired to – the best article in the market.

NOTES

1. "To William Dean Howells," March 30, 1877, in *Henry James: Letters*, ed. Leon Edel (Cambridge, Mass.: Harvard University Press, 1975), Vol. II, p. 105.

2. R. P. Blackmur, ed., *The Art of the Novel* (New York: Scribners, 1934), p. 37. Further references are given in the text in parentheses as (*AN*).

3. "To William Dean Howells," October 24, 1876, in Edel, ed., *Henry James: Letters*, Vol. II, p. 70.

4. Henry James, *The American*, ed. James W. Tuttleton (New York: Norton, 1978), p. 160.

5. "To William Dean Howells," March 30, 1877, in Edel, ed., *Henry James: Letters*, Vol. II, p. 105.

6. *The Sociology of Georg Simmel*, ed. Kurt H. Wolff (Glencoe, Ill: Free Press, 1950), p. 411.

7. *Henry James: Parisian Sketches*, ed. Leon Edel and Ilse Dusoir Lind (New York: Collier, 1961), p. 93.

8. *The Philosophy of Money* (London, 1978), p. 383.

9. A. de Pontmartin, "Semaines litteraires," *La Gazette de France*, June 11, 1865, quoted in T. J. Clark, *The Painting of Modern Life: Paris in the Art of Manet and His Followers* (New York: Knopf, 1985), p. 111.

10. "The Origin of Prostitution in Ancient Mesopotamia," *Signs* 11 (Winter 1986):253.

11. Cf. Gayle Rubin, "The Traffic in Women: Notes on the 'Political Economy' of Sex," in *Toward an Anthropology of Women*, ed. Rayna R. Reiter (New York: Monthly Review Press, 1975), pp. 57–210.

12. Cf. William Veeder, *Henry James: The Lessons of the Master* (Chicago: University of Chicago Press, 1975), pp. 118–19.

13. The most provocative treatment of these issues is Eve Kosofsky Sedgwick's "The Beast in the Closet: James and the Writings of Homosexual Panic," in *Sex, Politics, and Science in the Nineteenth-Century Novel*, ed. Ruth Bernard Yeazell (Baltimore: Johns Hopkins University Press,

1986). A contrasting view may be found in Alfred Habegger, *Gender, Fantasy and Realism in American Literature* (New York: Columbia University Press, 1982).

14. "To William Dean Howells," October 24, 1876, in Edel, ed., *Henry James: Letters,* Vol. II, p. 72.

15. Edel and Lind, ed., *Parisian Sketches,* p. 50.

16. Ibid., p. 32.

Physical Capital: *The American* and the Realist Body

MARK SELTZER

1. "Just as a Chair or Table"

ONE of the most telling passages in Harriet Beecher Stowe's *Uncle Tom's Cabin* (1852) appears just after Tom has been sold to his final owner, Simon Legree, and just before he has arrived at Legree's nightmarish plantation. The subject of this "middle passage" is what Stowe calls "one of the bitterest apportionments" of slavery – the slave's liability to be sold from a "refined family" from which he has acquired "the tastes and feelings which form the atmosphere of such a place" to the "coarsest and most brutal" master, and sold, moreover, "just as a chair or table, which once decorated the superb saloon comes, at last, battered and defaced, to the bar-room of some filthy tavern, or some low haunt of vulgar debauchery." But more significant for our purposes, it is just the uneasy pertinence of the analogy between slave and chair or table that leads Stowe, at this point, to reassert the absolute difference that forms the more fundamental subject of her story: put simply, the difference between a person and a thing. "The great difference is," Stowe goes on to state, "that the table and chair cannot feel, and the *man* can."[1]

What is remarkable about this passage, of course, is not what it says but rather the perverse necessity of stating what ought to go without saying, a perversity necessitated by slavery's monstrous denial of the "great difference" between a sentient person and a thing like a chair. Yet it is just the self-evident status of this difference that Stowe's novel ultimately and disturbingly suggests is possibly somewhat too self-evident. Indeed, if the great difference between a person and a thing is that one feels and the other doesn't, then Stowe's not at all atypical description, earlier in the novel, of the motherly Quaker Rachel Halliday's chair presents something of a problem, since the description also violates this difference, albeit from the other side:

> It had a turn for quacking and squeaking, – that chair had, – either from having taken cold in early life, or from some asthmatic affection, or perhaps from nervous derangement . . . old Silas Halliday often declared it was as good as any music to him, and the children all avowed that they wouldn't miss of hearing mother's chair for anything in the world. For why? for twenty years or more, nothing but loving words, and gentle moralities, and motherly loving kindness, had come from that chair. (*UTC,* p. 215)

There is certainly nothing very startling about such everyday animism. But clearly, such an indifferent transgressing of what Stowe sets up as the founding difference between persons and property poses a problem in a novel originally subtitled "The Man That Was a Thing" and centered on representing "the feelings of living property." And although the uncertainty about the relations between persons and things is nowhere more insistent than in a novel about the peculiarities of slavery, I want further to suggest that such an uncertainty characterizes not merely *Uncle Tom's Cabin* but also the middle and later nineteenth-century American novel generally.

"I never saw so much expression in an inanimate thing before," the narrator of Charlotte Perkins Gilman's story "The Yellow Wallpaper" (1892) recalls about her "plain furniture": "there was one chair that always seemed like a strong friend."[2] There is something of a continuity between Stowe's philosophy of furniture and the personifications of her grandniece Gilman, and the continuity indicates more than simply a family resemblance. It indicates, I think, one of the central subjects of the American novel in this period: a concern with the status of subjects, as persons and as living property, and, collaterally, with the status of material things, such as chairs or tables or, more anxiously, bodies.

In these pages I investigate this configuration of relations – relations of bodies, economies, and forms of representation – in the novel. My primary focus is Henry James's *The American,* a novel that enacts, in an almost diagrammatic fashion, a set of relations, relays, and displacements between the bodily and the economic. My treatment of the novel centers on the ways in which social and economic practices are physically embodied, and with the ways in which imperatives of embodiment and personification constitute the novel's account of the "commercial person." At one extreme, this imperative of embodiment appears as a problem, at once literary and economic, of putting persons, meanings, and values "on paper," and I am concerned with the novel's uneasy investments in what writers and economists in the later nineteenth century described as the American "paper system." Most generally, I attempt to define what I would call the logistics or *social logistics* of James's novel, the practical and exigent deployment and disposition of persons, things, and representations. My concern is with how both James's contradictory account of the character of the "commercial person" and the novel's contradictory and radically unstable styles of representation – "romance" and "realism" – engage such a logistics, and moreover, with how these contradictions and instabilities become functional within the novel, at once registering and securing the complicated nexus of bodies and commerce that make up James's account of "physical capital."

2. "Physical Capital"

Near the close of *The American*, just before Christopher Newman returns for his last brief visit to Paris, there is a small scene that condenses a rich cluster of the novel's thematic concerns. Newman, returning to New York, "sat for three days in the lobby of his hotel, looking out through a huge wall of plate-glass at the unceasing stream of pretty girls in Parisian-looking dresses, undulating past with little parcels nursed against their neat figures."[3] Newman's positioning as spectator concisely invokes one of the most explicit links in the novel – an association of a way of seeing and a desire for acquisition or "glory of possession" (118). More specifically, the scene's association of girl watching and window shopping is scarcely surprising in a novel that conceives of sexual relations in terms of, and only in terms of, market relations, the marriage market or prostitution. Newman's desire for Claire de Cintré is expressed as a desire "to possess, in a word, the best article in the market" (44), and this desire appears preeminently as a seeing at once appropriative and aesthetic. The commercial, sexual, and aesthetic are inextricably conjoined by a certain mode of looking in the novel.

On the one side, *The American* insists that aesthetic and sexual matters are not outside of or opposed to the economic, but rather are bound up with it, through and through and from the start; on the other, the novel represents precisely a reaction against this recognition, much as Newman considers his attempt "to pick up aesthetic entertainment in Europe," whether girls or pictures, as a "strong reaction against questions exclusively commercial" (301), an "indifference" to the "Exchange" (303). Just such a double attitude is played out in this scene and on both sides of the huge wall of glass.

For one thing, it is not hard to see that the "unceasing stream" of girls makes for a certain crisis of distinctions. The scene involves not merely Newman's looking but also an endlessly proliferating stream of look-alikes, of "pretty girls" in "Parisian-looking dresses." Clearly, this stream of imitation Parisiennes serves as a metonym of the traffic of, and in, women that the novel represents. But most striking about the passage is what might be called the "undulating" of the description itself, the wavering between registers of its terms. I am referring not simply to the mass production of copies – of fashionable imitations – that makes possible this flowing line of pretty girls, nor simply to the way in which the consumerism of these parcel-carrying girls doubles the acquisitive watching of the man on the other side of the window. The specular doubling here is a sort of intermirroring, a multiplying of looking and copying – the representational or mimetic "style" that figures the production and consumption of commodities in the later nineteenth-century novel. One might say that the large plate-glass works as a looking glass – at once window and mirror – of desire even as it unsteadily demarcates and partitions positions of seeing and being seen, of power and possession. The glass "wall" separates the places of the watching subject and the objects that consolidate but also work to multiply and therefore to disperse his position as consumer. The plate-glass thus functions at once as a wall and as a transparent and permeable surface of exchange; and the stream of girls functions as both the object and the objectification of a general consumerist vision – a consumerism that pivots on the "neat figure" of the pretty girl.[4]

But the production of copies also operates in a somewhat different and more startling form in this passage, and in a manner that makes even more explicit the exchanges of sexual and economic registers in the novel. Is there a great difference, for instance, between the bodies of these pretty girls and the "neat figures" of a commercial taking-into-account? And is there not something of a resemblance between the "little parcels" they carry and other sorts of bundles these commodities seem to displace, living property "nursed against" these figures? The bodily and the economic, one form of reproduction and another, are almost interchangeable here, two ways of saying the same thing.

Stated as simply as possible, *The American* poses the problem of the relation between persons and things by way of a consideration of what James calls the "commercial person." The indecisiveness concerning the status of reproduction, mechanical and biological, and of the relations between bodies and figures is crucially significant in a novel that, for instance, introduces its main character by describing his body as "physical capital" (18) and presents the "private" domain of the embodied subject alternatively as a "public" affair of the market. For Newman, James notes in passing,

> handling money in public was on the contrary positively disagreeable . . . he had a sort of personal modesty about it, akin to what he would have felt about making a toilet before spectators. But just as it was a gratification to him to be handsomely dressed, just so it was a private satisfaction to him (he enjoyed it very clandestinely) to have interposed, pecuniarily, in a scheme of pleasure. (p. 197)

Hence, although *The American* posits emphatic oppositions between the personal and the commercial, between private and public, between the subject and material objects, it is precisely the interpenetration or even reversibility and exchangeability of these terms that the novel enacts. "His book overflows with the description of material objects," James observes in 1875 in a review of Taine's *Notes on Paris*, "of face and hair, shoulders and arms, jewels, dresses, and furniture."[5] What the realist inventory of physical capital is indifferent to, it would appear, is a difference, great or even small, between the embodied self and the material object.

3. "A Person not a Picture"

The realist novel, I am suggesting, is everywhere underwritten by anxieties about living property and, collaterally, by anxieties about what counts as a person or subject. "Ideas of persons and things, all had dissolved and lost coherence and were seething together in apparently irretrievable chaos," Edward Bellamy not at all atypically observes in *Looking Backward* (1888).[6] *The American* plays out the problem of the relation between persons and things, and between the body and capital, in terms of a certain logic, or better, *logistics* of representation. By this I mean not simply that the novel focuses on the "topic" of living property, although this topic clearly preoccupies the novel; or simply that the novel repeatedly represents scenes of representation, copying, and reproduction, although such an insistence is also clear enough. Rather, the novel points to the way in which this topic (living property) and this recurrent scene (of representation) are inextricably linked in the realist text. *The American* does not simply represent the problematic relation of persons and objects but represents it *as* a problem of representation, imitation, and reproduction. This is the case not because the novel is "really" about representation but because representation in the novel is *already* about the relations of physical capital that I have begun to trace. What has made these relations almost unreadable is the virtually automatic critical tendency to view the obsessive return to scenes of representation in the realist novel as an indication of some internal critical and self-reflexive distance between the novel's topics and its techniques, as if the representation of a subject in the novel automatically placed that subject, as it were, in quotation marks. What troubles *The American*, however, is not a critical difference between aesthetic and social or physical forms of reproduction but rather what amounts to the collapsing of the difference between these forms.

The American in fact begins by invoking notions of copying or reproduction in the context of desires at once commercial, sexual, and aesthetic. And in this scene, as in the scene of the glass wall we have just considered, the tight specularity of these desires is most compelling. Newman, having "taken serene possession" of the scene in the Louvre that opens the novel, observes not merely all the pictures but "all the copies that were going forward around them." These copies include the copyists themselves: "innumerable young women in irreproachable toilets who devote themselves, in France, to the propagation of masterpieces" (17). The propagation of copies by young women within the museum again peripherally invokes another kind of reproduction. Just outside the museum, Newman's look is insistently drawn to groups of "white-capped nurses, seated along the benches," as if arranged in efficient and productive rows, and "offering to their infant charges the amplest facilities for nutrition" (29). The novel juxtaposes one form of propagation and another and insists on Newman's interest: he looked "at the nurses and babies. . . . Newman continued to look at the nurses and babies" (30, 31).

What is particularly marked, then, in this opening scene is a generalized fascination with imitation and reproduction, and this fascination with imitation is part of the more general account of *representation* that the novel proceeds by invoking. Newman, James observes, likes copies: "if the truth must be told, he had often admired the copy much more than the original" (17). On one level, Newman's fascination with the making of copies is not difficult to account for. If, as he remarks to M. de Bellegarde, "Manufactures are what I care most about" (124), this interest in "making" (a term, in its variants, consistently associated with Newman) can be seen as part of the commercial initiatives that Newman represents. As David M. Potter, for instance, observes in his *People of Plenty: Economic Abundance and the American Character*, "European radical thought is prone to demand that the man of property be stripped of his carriage and his fine clothes. But American radical thought is likely to insist, instead, that the ordinary man is entitled to mass-produced copies, indistinguishable from the originals."[7] One might say, then, that Newman likes copies because making is what he cares most about – making money and things, but also and crucially, making persons, the physical capital of the self-made man.

Newman's admiration for copies can thus be seen as defining, at least in part, the representative "type" of the commercial person. But James's concern with the character of the commercial person, as represented and as representative, goes "all the way down" and the problem becomes precisely: What is the relation between a person and what he or she represents or personifies? More specifically, how is character, in this account, related to the more general type or original of which he or she appears as a copy? Newman is introduced as an embodiment of a particular "American type" (18) – as an instance of what "he 'represented'" (43); he expresses his "national origin" with an "almost ideal completeness" (18).[8] How, then, is the problem of representation itself, in *The American*, perhaps a local instance of a more general "commercial" economy of copies and originals, and how is such an ideal of representation instanced by the practice of the novel itself?

This linking of aesthetic and commercial economies of representation can perhaps be clarified by looking more closely at how James represents the relation between a picture and a person in the novel. Newman's admiration for copies points to what James describes as Newman's aesthetic "baffle[ment]," a confounding of copy and original allied to "the damning fault (as we have lately discovered it to be) of confounding the merit of the artist with that of his work" (19). But Newman's confusion of the copyist Noémie Nioche's "merit" with her work turns out to have somewhat more significant implications than at first appears. Noémie's painting of the Madonna resembles the making up of a prostitute ("she deposited a rosy blotch in the middle of the Madonna's cheek" [20]), and the "copy" and the "beautiful subject" she offers for sale implicitly refer, of course, both to her painting and to *herself* as a remarkable, and marketable, imitation of the type of the "perfect Parisienne."

The confounding of a person and a picture enacted here poses again the problematic relation of persons and objects, this time in terms of the aesthetic object itself. From one perspective, that of a certain formalism, the confounding of a person and a picture is simply a mistake, a "damning fault"; from another, it is just this mistake that, in effect, turns a portrait into a character, into a person defined not by freedom from representation but in fact

characterized, in both senses, by what he or she imitates or represents. The problem is, as Tristram remarks, that in Paris "they
imitate, you know, so deucedly well . . . you can't tell the things
[original and imitation] apart" (28). The confounding of person
and picture that the novel here ironically disavows is thus itself
part of the "faulty" account of representation upon which the
"story" of the novel depends, and this story is itself always a story
about the commerce in persons.

The most explicit invocation of this logistics of character and
story occurs in the second major scene in the museum (chapter
11), Newman's meeting with Noémie to check on "the progress of
his copies," which is also, in the meeting of Valentin de Bellegarde
and Noémie, the "progress of the young lady herself" (129). What
centers the scene, it will be recalled, is not Noémie's copying but
rather, in response to Valentin's critique, her defacement of the
picture:

> "I know the truth – I know the truth," Mademoiselle Noémie
> repeated. And dipping a brush into a clot of red paint, she drew a
> great horizontal daub across her unfinished picture.
> "What is that? asked Newman.
> Without answering, she drew another long crimson daub, in a
> vertical direction, down the middle of her canvas, and so, in a
> moment, completed the rough indication of a cross. "It is the sign of
> the truth," she said at last. (p. 133)

The passage proceeds by juxtaposing two different but interdependent accounts of representation and by staging a certain oscillation
between them. The defacement or marking out of the picture becomes a mark or sign; the crossing out of the portrait becomes a
cross, a form of iconic writing, "the sign of the truth." There is a
good deal more to be said about this astonishingly condensed
representation of forms of marking – of inscription as picture or as
writing, as sign and as mere material "daub." The tensions between picture and writing and between mere marks and legible
signs, I argue, are crucial to the problem of representation in the
novel. For the moment, however, I am more interested in the
responses that Noémie's crossing out evokes here. Newman complains that Noémie's daubs "have spoiled your picture." But Valentin's very different commentary concisely enunciates what I

have called the logistics of story in *The American*. "I like it better that way than as it was before," Valentin declares: "Now it is more interesting. It tells a story. Is it for sale, mademoiselle?" For Valentin, Noémie's defacement of her portrait is a move from picture to narrative, and the move from portrait to story also and necessarily entails a story of exchange — "Is it for sale?" — and a commerce embodied in persons — " 'Everything I have is for sale,' said Mademoiselle Noémie."

What this passage provisionally indicates is thus an almost schematic configuration of relations or a set of relays between commercial exchanges, persons, and stories. Put even more schematically, the passage indicates that to get rid of the commercial is to get rid of what counts as a person, and to eliminate what counts as a person is to eliminate what for James is the very principle of a story — the exchanges and relations that, as James expresses it in his preface to *Roderick Hudson*, "stop nowhere." Another way of saying this is that the difference between a person and a picture in *The American* is the difference between a story and a portrait, or, in accordance with the names that James gives to these different representational practices, the difference between the novel and the romance. What characterizes the romance, as James argues in his preface to *The American*, is a fantasy of unrelatedness. The romance, as opposed to the novel, consists of a certain "liberated" "kind of experience," of "experience disengaged, disembroiled, disencumbered," of experience, above all, relieved of "the inconvenience of a *related*, a measurable state . . . at large and unrelated" (11).

If story consists in relations, it is precisely a sacrifice of story that *The American* risks or in fact advertises: The novel explicitly turns, in its second half and with the breaking of the engagement, from the entanglement of relations embodied in the commercial person to a form of representation that is something like (and indeed literalizes) the disengaged and unrelated state that James calls "a page torn out of romance" (276). Yet the very turning away from forms of relation and engagement, the very turn from novel to romance and from a story of exchange to a romance exempt from both story and exchange, is not finally supported by the "confounding" practice we have begun to trace in the Jamesian text.

140

The radical oppositions that James advertises talk past and work to disavow the radically different story he tells.[9] What *The American* finally reveals is not an opposition between romance and novel or between related states and a fantasy of unrelatedness and autonomy. Rather, romance and novel, autonomy and relatedness, finally appear as the two sides of the coin that James calls physical capital.

4. Romance and Novel

One way of clarifying what is involved here is by turning to the novelistic practice that lies back of James's diagrammatic consideration of problems of relations and representation in *The American.* On the threshold of the meeting with Noémie that we have just glanced at, Newman remarks to Valentin that "I have in fact come to see a person and not a picture." In his study *Hawthorne,* written shortly after *The American,* James critically comments on the "light and vague" and "disembodied" typicality of the characters of Hawthorne's *The House of the Seven Gables:* "they are all pictures rather than persons."[10] The difference between a picture and a person posited here functions also for James as a difference between romance and novelistic forms, and between the versions of the self and of representation that these rival forms entail.

The opposition of the "romance" to the "novel" continues, of course, to govern critical treatments of American fiction, most basically as a way of locating the "positions" of this fiction – in the simplest terms, positions for or against the worldly or "social" and, more particularly, for or against the social and representational styles of capitalism. What such an oppositional logic fails to account for, however, in protecting the differences between these forms and positions, are not merely the highly complicated ways in which these very differences and oppositions are promoted and deployed within the fictions, romantic or realistic, themselves but also the difficulties involved in aligning particular literary forms with particular and exclusive positions, for or against – as if a form and an ideology neatly reflected each other, as if, for instance, the Romance said "no" to capitalism, the Novel "yes." My point is not that literary texts are position free, or that the literary text, in saying at once "yes and no," moves beyond ideology into the territory of undecidability. My point is, rather, and with particular reference to the middle and later nineteenth-century American romance and novel, that the recalcitrant oppositions within and between these forms can best be understood in terms of a certain logistics in which these opposed forms and positions each "have their place." A brief consideration of Hawthorne's *The House of the Seven Gables* (1851) can perhaps clarify the *emergence* of such a logistics − the relations of the bodily and the economic that James adapts and revises in *The American* − and take this discussion of commercial persons, embodiment, and representation a step further.

It does not require much pressure to see that Hawthorne's novel traces a transition from aristocratic to bourgeois models of the family − as Hawthorne expresses it, "the state of the family had changed."[11] Nor is it hard to see that this transition is bound up with the problem of the body. The novel focuses on the body as the locus of history and meaning both − on the body *as* embodiment. Hawthorne's portrayal of the aristocratic Pyncheons' "ancestral" chickens, for instance, economically exemplifies this insistence on the body. The chickens function as a "symbol of the life of the old house," "embodying its interpretation" even as they "embodied the traditionary peculiarities of their whole line of progenitors." The smallest of the chickens has "aggregated into itself the ages": All of its ancestors "were squeezed into its little body" (151). But if Hawthorne is here sketching a sort of protogenetic fantasy or quasi-biological account of how something like original sin could be passed on from generation to generation, "squeezed into" suc-cessive shapes and "reproducing itself in successive generations" (240), it is necessary to emphasize that the novel's original trans-gression has to do with property and its transmission.[12] What focuses this nexus of property and the body is the practice of the family.

The small body of the ancestral chicken represents what Haw-thorne calls aristocratic "transmission"; Phoebe Pyncheon's "nice little body" (79) centers Hawthorne's treatment of the new "re-publican" family of conjugality and domesticity. And if "transmis-sion," of property and identity, defines the aristocratic body, what

Hawthorne calls "communication," "circulation," and "intercourse" define its bourgeois successor. It is not simply that Phoebe, through a sort of "homely witchcraft" (72), converts the house of the seven gables into a home, but that this conversion involves a new relation between persons and objects and between objects such as bodies. Phoebe's little body exerts a "force" that has the capacity "to bring out the hidden capabilities of things around [her]" (71). Her "influence" is manifested, for instance, in "the effect which she produced on a character of so much more mass than her own" (137), an effect, at once spiritual and physical, of magnetic attraction. Phoebe's assumption of the office of housewife involves "not so much assuming the office as attracting it to herself, by the magnetism of innate fitness" (76). What characterizes Phoebe's rearrangement of the relations of persons and things is, above all, a power of personification, a "natural magic" that operates as a species of animism.[13] Finally, this circulation or communication between persons and things involves also an eroticization of everyday relations. Phoebe's "human intercourse" (141) animates bodies and objects and alters the very "air" of the house of the seven gables: "she impregnated it" (143).

From one point of view, Phoebe's impregnating intercourse resolves the problematic relation between persons and things in the novel by creating what has familiarly been called the "separate sphere" of domesticity and conjugality: the sexualized, privatized space of the new state of the family, the romance of the "new Eden" that "separated Phoebe and [Holgrave] from the world" (305).[14] But from another, the animistic economy of the new family appears not as separate from but in fact as entailing the very worldliness that it seems to oppose. Phoebe's homely magic is implicitly associated with an apparently very different kind of witchcraft in the novel. The "little circlet of the school-boy's copper coin" — the first income in Hepzibah Pyncheon's little shop — communicates a certain "galvanic impulse." The small copper, "dim and lusterless though it was, with the small services which it had been doing, here and there about the world had proved a talisman. . . . It was as potent, and perhaps endowed with the same kind of efficacy, as a galvanic ring!" (52). An animating magnetism, a power of circulation and intercourse, characterizes

both Phoebe's domestic influence and the witchcraft of the marketplace itself. From this rather different point of view, what Phoebe's little body is an embodiment of is the circulating medium of
capital itself.[15]

On the one side, aristocratic transmission in *The House of the
Seven Gables* is explicitly aligned with romance and portrait and,
collaterally, with death or death-in-life; on the other, communication, circulation, and intercourse are functions of what Hawthorne
calls the "business of life." It is precisely the interplay and transit
between these two "sides" that defines Hawthorne's practice: The
communication of stories is, for Hawthorne, inevitably the "op-
en[ing of] a door that communicated with the shop" (36). The
"solution" to the anxious relation between persons and things
that Hawthorne devises is a commerce embodied in persons, a
story of physical capital. The point, of course, is not finally that the
differences between the family and the marketplace, between private and public, or between romantic and novelistic imperatives
are eradicated, but rather that both spheres are premised on and
work to sustain a certain account of the relations of bodies and
things – the relations of living property. The story of physical
capital involves not an intrinsic difference between public and
private or between "the sexual" and "the economic," but precisely the relays – the circulation and communication – progressively elaborated between these "separate" registers. Put simply, these differences form part of and are in fact dependent on and
produced by the more general economy of bodies and powers that
I have been indicating here.

I am suggesting, in returning to *The American,* that the Jamesian
opposition between romance and novel – between the unrelated
and autonomous representations and persons that James aligns
with the romance and the related states and commercial persons
that James treats as the subject of the novel – is an instance of this
general economy of bodies and powers. Clearly, James's characterization of the romance, and of its critical difference from the
novel, works to protect the antinomies between private and public
accounts of persons and things and between rival forms of representation. In what follows, I reexamine, from a somewhat different perspective, these opposed discourses of the self and of repre-

sentation, and indicate the ways in which they in fact constitute the two-sided or double discourse of living property.

5. "The Paper System"

Hawthorne's *The House of the Seven Gables,* a sort of halfway house, works to conserve the private and separate sphere (of the family and the self) even as it reveals the dependence of the very notion of the "private" on the newly dominant relations of the market.[16] James's version of the confrontation between the aristocratic family and the business of life would seem to rewrite *The House of the Seven Gables* in reverse: If Hawthorne represents the opening of a communication with the business of life as a shift toward the novelistic, *The American* explicitly turns, with the rupture of relations between Newman and Claire, from novel to romance and melodrama. "The recurrent Jamesian subject," Leo Bersani has observed, "is freedom" and it is in the name of such a radical (literary) freedom and autonomy of character that, as we have seen, James in his preface defends this turn to romance.[17] But what *The American* reveals is the way in which the Jamesian values of freedom and autonomy (the values of romance) forward and are forwarded by the very (novelistic) economizing of relations they seem to oppose. The oppositional logic James advertises finally takes the form of a functional, if not quite loyal, opposition: not an opposition between romance and exchange but what amounts to a romance of capitalism itself.

Not surprisingly, this double discourse is most apparent in James's account of the commercial person, Christopher Newman. What characterizes Newman is, most of all, his "freedom" and his autonomous and unrelated state, his "almost ideal completeness" (18). Newman's freedom is centrally a freedom *from* family. "And are you perfectly free?" Noémie asks Newman:

> "How do you mean, free?"
> "You have nothing to bother you — no family, no wife, no *fiancée?*"
> "Yes, I am tolerably free." (p. 62)

Paradoxically enough, Newman's account of marriage is not at all at odds with such a "tolerable" freedom. What Newman proposes to Claire is marriage not as a "losing [of] your freedom" (113) but precisely as its achievement: "you ought to be perfectly free and marriage will make you so" (115). This is in part because Newman sees marriage as an extrication from family relations, expressing not a desire to "come into" the family but rather the desire "to take Madame de Cintré out of it" (144): "I want to marry your sister," Newman informs the Marquis, "that's all. . . . I am not marrying you, you know, sir" (143). But this is also because Newman's version of alliance calls for *dis*connection. For Newman, the members of the family are "very different parties": "I see no connection between you" (250–1).[18]

At one extreme, Newman's paradoxical account of relations conserves the very values of romance that the commercial person seems to threaten; at another, however, this twin form of alliance and disconnection – of "different parties" – is a striking instance of the logistics of physical capital. More specifically, the severing of relations between Newman and Claire is a consequence of the breaking of a promise. Indeed, the making or breaking of promises underwrites the plot of the novel, from Newman's "solemn promise" to Claire to defer speaking of marriage for six months (115) to his attempt to restore relations by signing a "paper promising never to come back to Europe" (219). The promise, however, functions in two very different codes in the novel. Whereas the first involves the aristocratic code of honor (aligned, in the novel, with vengeance and the duel), the second involves precisely the two-sided form of relating different parties, while maintaining their difference and autonomy, that defines the commercial person (a "liberal" form aligned with the "bargain" and the law). " 'If you stick to your own side of the contract we shall not quarrel; that is all I ask of you,' said Newman" (147). What looks from one point of view like a dishonorable breaking of a promise appears, from another, as a breach of contract. The model of the *contract* defines the novel's paradoxical economy of relation.

As the social historian Thomas L. Haskell argues in a recent study of capitalism and interests, there is a close connection between the emergence of the "norm of promise keeping" and the triumph of capitalism.[19] A contract, of course, represents a legal exchange of promises and, as Haskell suggests, the "growing re-

liance on mutual promises, or contractual relations, in lieu of relations based on status, custom, or traditional authority comes very
close to the heart of what we mean by 'the rise of capitalism.' "[20]
One consequence of this transformation in the character of relations is a new characterization of the subject. The task becomes, in
Nietzsche's terms, "to breed an animal *with the right to make promises*" – that is, an individual defined by the radical freedom of will
that contractual promises presuppose ("I will") and by a power
over circumstance, a standing security for the enforcement of one's
will, that the keeping of promises requires ("I must").[21] A contract requires, in other words, the "sovereign individual" defined
at once by the sovereignty of his or her will and by an obligation to
abjure willfulness. The "possessive individual" of a contract is, to
paraphrase William James, possessed by his possessions. That is to
say, what defines the freedom and autonomy of the individual, the
principle of "identity" over time and circumstance that makes
promise keeping possible – the ability, or what Newman calls the
"duty," of "resembling oneself" (158) – is the determination of
the individual by his or her determinations.[22]

To "have a character," in Benjamin Franklin's formulation, is to
be a subject who can make good on his promises. And if Franklin
is invoked more than once in *The American* (32, 146) as Newman's
archetype, this is because the self-made character of the commercial person in the novel is an embodiment of the promissory relations of contract I have sketched. I will be returning, in the final
part of this essay, to some further consequences of such an account
of capitalism and the problematic relation of will and determinism
that it entails. For the moment, however, it is necessary to recon-
sider in more detail the ways in which the two-sided discourse of
physical capital effectively informs not merely the novel's representation of the subject but also the novel's almost schematic treatment of the subject of representation and embodiment itself.

The commercial person, we have seen, admires copies, often
more than originals; he is fascinated by reproductions and representations. Moreover, the commercial person's identity, or self-
identity, depends on representation: That identity is guaranteed by
the imperative of resembling oneself, as a copy corresponds to its
original. But such a dependence of identity on resemblance – such

147

an equation of the self and its representations – must be guaranteed, in turn, by a certain restricted account of resemblance and representation. Self-identity, for Newman, is a "duty" and not a "given," and what this points to is the possibility of a discrepancy and not a simple correspondence between the self and its embodiments, or rather, within the self as embodiment. It is precisely this discrepancy that Newman disavows. And it is just the implications and vicissitudes of such a disavowal for the practice of the realist novel that *The American* displays.

Newman insists on an ideal correspondence between the self and its representations, an insistence perhaps clearest in his discomfort with the "queer" gap between public and private that defines the aristocratic form of life. Claire's house, for instance, presents "to the outer world a face as impassive and as suggestive of the concentration of privacy within as the blank walls of Eastern seraglios. Newman thought it a queer way for rich people to live; his ideal of grandeur was a splendid facade, diffusing its brilliancy outward too, irradiating hospitality" (50). What disturbs Newman is the discrepancy between outer face and interior. Similarly, what Newman finds "really infernal" about Mademoiselle Noémie is the contrast between "her appearance" and her acts: "She looked 'lady-like'" (175). Above all, the desire to eliminate a difference between what things look like and what they embody appears in an aversion to the category of the secret. "Secrets were, in themselves, hateful things," for Newman: "He felt, himself, that he was an antidote to oppressive secrets; what he offered [Claire] was, in fact, above all things a sunny immunity from the need of having any" (151). As Newman expresses it, "I don't like mysteries" (195).

Newman desires a natural "fit" between outer face and private interior – a sort of physiognomy – that effectively eliminates the difference between outside and inside, public and private. In fact, a concern with physiognomy, and with the legibility of the interior on the surface of the body that it implies, is frequently invoked in the novel.[23] But such a natural legibility of meaning appears also in the remarkable accounts that James gives of Newman's relation to language, reading, and writing. "The use that I want to make of your secret," Newman tells Mrs. Bread, is to make it public, or, more precisely, as Mrs. Bread expresses it, "you want to publish [it]" (257). The desire to publish the family's secret paper reiterates in part Newman's dislike of mysteries. But it invokes as well the related but more fundamental questions that the novel takes up with an extraordinary explicitness: What does it mean to make marks on paper, to read them, and to publish them? What is the relation between language, marking, or writing and the meaning each represents or embodies? Finally, and from a different perspective, what is the relation between this problematic of representation and the logistics of embodiment that, as we have seen, defines the general economy of physical capital?

The novel, I am suggesting, posits or at least promotes an identity between what things look like and what they mean, and such an identification is most evident, in *The American*, in James's insistence on Newman's natural and even instinctual relation to language and meaning. Newman, James observes near the start of the novel, "understood no French," and yet he "apprehended, by a natural instinct, the meaning of the young woman's phrase" (21). Repeatedly, Newman "emerged from dialogues in foreign tongues, of which he had, formally, not understood a word, in full possession of the particular fact he had desired to ascertain" (66). Newman's relation to "philological processes" is a relation to physiological processes: "ascertaining those mysterious correlatives of his familiar English vocables" was "simply a matter of . . . muscular effort on his own part" (24–5). Newman's linguistic materialism equates sounds or material signs with meanings, and if he "formally" does not understand a word, it is a certain formalism by which material things resemble the meanings they embody that defines Newman's philology.

Yet this natural account of meaning is at once opposed to and coupled with a very different account of representation in the novel. In my earlier discussion of the scene in the museum in which Noémie crosses out her picture, I suggested that this scene condenses an opposition between portrait and story by implicitly staging an opposition between representing as drawing and representing as a kind of writing; the crossing out of the picture becomes a legible sign, "the sign of the truth," at once icon and mark on canvas. This scene, and the novel generally, counterposes two versions of meaning: at one extreme, a radical correspondence by which things, like portraits, look like what they represent, and, at the other, a principle of discrepancy by which signs, like writing, represent what they don't look like.

It's not a matter of the novel's taking sides, choosing one version or the other; rather, these two sides form the opposed surfaces of a single formation. Newman insists on a correspondence between what persons look like and what they are, between outward forms and the meanings they embody, and between forms of language or writing and what they represent. But it is the capitalist financier, of course, who relies centrally on the *discrepancies* between "things themselves" and the values or meanings they represent. He relies not on a correspondence theory of value but on the vicissitudes and excesses of exchange and speculation that, for instance, make possible Newman's astonishingly rapid money making. This money making remains one of the "disliked" and disavowed secrets of the novel. It is this secret and principle of discrepancy both that Newman disavows in his horse-car conversion from the "Exchange" and that James collaterally disowns in the horse-car discovery of the subject of his "romance," as he relates it in his preface (2). But the advertisement of such a disowning accounts neither for Newman's subsequent actions as commercial person nor for James's own policies of representation: It is just the discrepancy between what things look like and what they represent that, as we have seen, makes possible stories and persons in this novel. In all, the story of physical capital in *The American* involves precisely this double account of representation, a twin emphasis nowhere clearer than in James's own version of what was called, in the middle and later nineteenth century, the American "paper system."

Certainly, one of the novel's most explicit instances of these contradictory but ineradicably coupled styles of representation occurs in the scene in which Newman reads the "scrap of white paper" that contains the "secret" of the Bellegarde family. But even to call this scene a scene of reading may be to proceed a bit too quickly. Newman, James writes, "pulled out the paper and quickly unfolded it. It was covered with pencil-marks, which at first, in the feeble light, seemed indistinct. But Newman's fierce curiosity forced a meaning from the tremulous signs. The English

150

of them was as follows" (268). What is foregrounded in this somewhat perverse passage is a hesitating of the act of reading, and,
more precisely, an emphasis on the recalcitrant physicality of writing and reading — on the unfolding of a scrap of paper, on the
indistinctness of the penciled marks on the paper, on a translation,
in several senses, of marks into signs that equates construing
meaning with its forceful extraction from shifting, but also trem-
bling, signs. It is not simply that James insists on relations of force
and meaning, or even that the novel is not at all scandalized (as
recent maps of reading as misreading tend to be) by such relations.
Rather, the passage enacts in miniature a minimalist version of the
double account of representation I have been describing, bringing
into the closest proximity the contradictory insistencies of materiality and meaning. As in James's description of Tom Tristram's
stroll past the Veronese, the American "vaguely looking at it, but
much too near to see anything but the grain of the canvas" (26),
reading — or looking — in this passage comes close to coming too
close to mere marks on paper.

Such a reductive or minimalist effect characterizes the final
chapters of *The American:* The story of capital and embodiment
turns increasingly to paper itself. I am referring in part to the
obsessive proliferation of images of papers, writing, and reading
toward the end of the novel. One finds here not merely an emphasis on the "marquis's manuscript" (267) as the "little paper"
(274), as "a scrap of white paper" (268), as "the paper — the
paper" (265); nor merely a reiterated concern with reading and
writing ("he read it. He had more than time to read it" [283];
"Wait till she reads the paper!" [285]). One finds as well a turning
of acts and bodies to paper: "Newman made a movement as if he
were turning over the page of the novel" (262); "her thin lips
curved like scorched paper" (281); "he turned to the marquis,
who was terribly white — whiter than Newman had ever seen
anyone out of a picture. 'A paper . . .'" (282). And finally, one
finds a minimalism that equates the consuming of paper and of the
novel itself. Even as Newman's burning of the little scrap of white
paper is a way to "close the book and put it away" (306), the
representation of the paper's consumption and the reader's consumption of James's representation are made to collate perfectly in

the novel's final sentence: "Newman instinctively turned to see if the little paper was in fact consumed; but there was nothing left of it" (309). The slight hesitation of James's "but" – marking the desire to see, or fear of seeing, nothing left to see – plangently reinforces this closing of the book.

It should by now hardly be surprising that the novel ends by drawing together a sort of consumerism and an account of representation. I have been arguing all along that the novel's return to scenes of representation and, more generally, its enactment of a logistics of embodiment indicate not simply a certain narrative self-reflexivity, not merely a critical reflection on representation, but finally something more: The novel is about embodiment because embodiment is already about physical capital, living property, and commercial persons. Newman's contractual self, for instance, is inseparable from the prominence of paper in the novel. To promise to leave Europe is to "sign a paper never to come back" (219); in his attempted bargain with the Bellegardes, "a simple *yes* or *no* on paper will do" (253); to enter into a relation, for Newman, is to sign a contract: "I never sign a paper without reading it first" (201). Newman's "business papers" (301), and the little piece of white paper he tries to bargain with, are finally instances of the same "paper system" that dominated later-nine-teenth-century concerns about money and representation both.

The novel opens in 1868 and appears in 1876, precisely the period of what has been called the "greenback era," the period in which the concern about how something like paper money could embody value became the dominant national issue, and a period in which precious and "hard" metals were also precious symbols of a medium of representation that looked like what it represented and paper money disturbingly represented what it didn't look like or feel like.[24] What was called the American "paper system" affected at once forms of money and forms of writing. As Marc Shell notes, "the apparently 'diabolical' 'interplay of money and mere writing to a point where the two be[come] confused' involves a general ideological development: the tendency of paper money to distort our 'natural' understanding of the relationship between symbols and thing."[25]

What is at work in *The American*, we have seen, is not so much a distortion of natural symbols by paper representations as the interplay of these rival modes of representation, an interplay that defines the discourse of physical capital. But I want, finally, to consider some of the problems involved in viewing these matters of embodiment and representation as themselves ultimately instances of – or indeed embodiments of – what, at bottom and in the final instance, are taken to be, in much recent work on literature and capitalism, determinant economic causes. George Eliot observes of Lydgate in *Middlemarch* (1871–2) that, in his youth, "he had no more thought of representing to himself how his blood circulated than how paper served instead of gold."[26] My concern to this point has been to investigate the configuration of representations that Eliot neatly condenses – a nexus of self-representations, representations of the body, monetary representation. The more general questions I want finally to ask are: What can the novelistic problematic of embodiment tell us about reading texts as instances or embodiments of social, economic, or political conditions or interests? What can it tell us about reading the self or subject as itself an instance, type, or embodiment?

6. "Something Stronger in Life than His Own Will"

The great difference between a person and a thing is, I have argued, one of the dominant subjects of the American novel in the third quarter of the nineteenth century, a period conveniently if roughly marked, at one end, by Stowe's investigation of America's "peculiar institution" of slavery – "one great market in bodies and souls" – and, at the other, by James's account of the "peculiar institutions of his native land" (289). In his preface to *The American*, James insistently aligns his own processes of composition with the relations of living property I have been outlining. At the outset, for instance, he links the "labour" of writing with the imperatives of an "economy of serialization" even as he treats this labor as a form of physical reproduction, a process of "germination" and gestation that makes "my conception concrete" through a "notable increase in weight" and an eventual "filling itself with light in that air" (1, 4, 3). The "happy development" of a subject – the way "things grow up and are formed" – is also an intensity of possession, the possession of another person as living property: "the intensity of the creative effort to get into the skin of the creature; the act of personal possession of one being by another at its completest" (7, 13).

The intent here has not so much been to disentangle these arrangements of bodies and economies as to indicate how such arrangements constitute the novel's account of physical capital. It is tempting to *explain* the novel's representation of the subject or self as an effect of newly emergent economic forms, specifically an effect of the market conditions of consumer capitalism. But the reading of the subject as an effect, instance, or embodiment of larger structures like the market is, we have seen, just what is at issue in the realist text. James represents Newman as defined at once by a radical freedom and as *"generally* characteristic of his type"* (Preface, 2). And whereas a certain account of realism, most powerfully elaborated by Georg Lukács, is premised on the view of character as general, characteristic, and typical, such a positing or taking for granted of (the possibility of) typicality or exemplarity also takes for granted a view of history that accounts for persons or events as instances or embodiments of larger determining historical forces and meanings. Such a view is perhaps not unlike Newman's fantasy of a natural and fully legible correspondence between persons and things and the meanings they embody. But the counterside of such a view is not hard to detect. Experiencing setbacks in his attempt to "wrest a fortune" from "impertinent force," Newman momentarily confronts a "mysterious something": "there seemed to him something in life stronger than his own will" (31–2). At work in the representation of the subject as at once body and embodiment – as physical capital – is just such a tension between free will and a version of force, and, more particularly, between the sovereign subject and a form or structure of economic determinism. It is this tension between subject and structure that I want finally to take up.[27]

In his study of capitalism and interests, Thomas L. Haskell provides a significant critique of what he calls the "social control thesis," the explanatory thesis that regards beliefs and acts as ultimately an index or reflex of economic or class interests. By this view, acts and beliefs flow from interests, and the effects of acts and beliefs are understood as the product of economic interests, whether these effects are consciously intended (the work of a visible hand) or self-deceptively or unconsciously intended (the work of an invisible one). For Haskell, the problem with the social control thesis is that it attributes a "greater degree of intention . . . than the evidence can substantiate." That is, this approach closes the gap between intentions and consequences, and between subjects and structures, but only by converting *unintended* consequences into *unconsciously intended* consequences.[28] "People know what they do," Michel Foucault remarked, and "they frequently know why they do what they do; but what they don't know is what what they do does." In his *Outline of a Theory of Practice*, the sociologist Pierre Bourdieu observes: "It is because subjects do not, strictly speaking, know what they are doing that what they do has more meaning than what they know." If Foucault's remark indicates an ineradicable gap between intentions and consequences, acts and meanings, Bourdieu's bridges this gap, but only by regarding apparently unintended consequences as unconsciously intended consequences. These two statements together could be taken to emblematize the rival accounts of the problem of subject and structure we have been considering.[29]

The solution for Haskell, among others, is to hold on to a version of economic determinism while eliminating the tie between economic structures and the intentions or interests of persons or classes. As he expresses it, the "rival scheme of explanation I advocate retains the claim that there is a 'process of determination,' but deliberately abandons the claim of intentionality." It quickly becomes clear, however, that the version of determination Haskell retains represents not an abandoning but in fact an even greater degree of intentionality. Haskell understands the rise of capitalism and what he calls the origins of the humanitarian sensibility in terms of "the forms of life the market encouraged," and throughout he emphasizes the "autonomous power of the market to shape character." What such a notion of the market's power involves, however, is precisely an attribution of intentionality to economic structures themselves. One might say that for Haskell the problem with the social control thesis is not that it attributes too much

155

intention but too little: If the market shapes the character of the subject of capitalism, this is because the market has itself become a subject, an agent with intentions, interests, and powers.[30]

Such a personifying of the market has, of course, a long history. As we have already seen, if in this account the dominance of the market makes persons into things, it also makes things, like tables, chairs, or markets, into persons. (Haskell's account, as we might by now expect, focuses on the problem of slavery). As Thorstein Veblen observes, in a chapter of *The Theory of the Leisure Class* called "The Belief in Luck," the "animistic sense of relations and things, that imputes a quasi-personal character to facts" survives side by side with an "industrial organization [that] assumes more and more of the character of a mechanism;" the animistic "habit of mind" survives, for instance, in the "modern reminiscence of the belief . . . in the guidance of an unseen hand."[31]

Stated very generally, recent accounts of the opposition between subject and structure have in effect reproduced, in the form of a theoretical neutralization, the coupled oppositions that define what we might call the "realist body" − the tensions between things and persons, mechanism and animism, materiality and meaning, the body and embodiment.[32] Not surprisingly, the still-governing opposition between the "constituent subject" and the "economic in the final instance" itself appears as a version of the twin determinations of the market: That is, if the market requires the "sovereign individual," the regularities and exchanges supported by the dominance of the impersonal mechanism of the "self-regulating market" are conducive not merely to a belief in determinism but also to a logic of infinite exchange and interconvertibility.[33]

These recent accounts have thus tended toward a theoretical duplication of this contradictory logic. For Haskell, for instance, the market imposes "forms of life," and the point is to abandon claims of intention and to trace these forms, "the subtle isomorphisms and homologies that arise from a cognitive style common to economic affairs."[34] Walter Benn Michaels, in a richly provocative study of late-nineteenth-century economic–literary relations, traces the ways in which an imperative of personification "constitutes the possibility of bourgeois economy." But for

Michaels, as for Haskell, "the whole point of [his] analysis . . . is, by subverting the primacy of the subject in literary history to subvert also the primacy of interest"; the aim is to locate "positions and their negations" in a logic or "double logic" and "in so doing to suggest one way of shifting the focus of literary history from the individual text and author to structures whose coherence, interest, and effect may be greater than that of either author or text."[35] Yet since this very opposition of subject to structure defines the "form" or "logic" of capitalism in both of these accounts, the question becomes: How do these moves from subject to structure avoid a *formalization* of the discourse of capitalism, avoid what amounts to, in effect, an economistic and structural logic of isomorphisms and reversible oppositions? How do they avoid the theorization effect or "radical formalism," for instance, that Michaels, here and elsewhere, has convincingly criticized?[36]

The alternative view that I have been indicating in this essay involves finally not a "logic" of physical capital but what I have called a "logistics." The arrangements of the bodily and the economic in the texts we have been considering do not occupy the logical space of infinitely reversible oppositions (although, as we have seen, there is an insistent tendency in the texts themselves to rewrite such a logistics in the form of a logical opposition — or rather, to "float" a normative logic against which a logistics functions); nor are they the embodiments of a determining and transcendent History. Rather, these arrangements occupy a contested space — what I have defined throughout as the *social logistics of physical capital.*[37] I have elsewhere argued that one alternative to the opposition of an empty voluntarism and an anonymous social mechanism might take the form of a "biopolitical analysis," an investigation of the subject's production at the point of intersection of bodily and economic practices.[38] The biopolitics we have been tracing in the novel involves what Pierre Bourdieu has called the fashioning of the "socially informed body," the adjustment and coordination of the dispositions of bodies and the exchanges of capital and meaning both.[39] Such a coordination operates in the most trivial and everyday practices and techniques, in all of those small adjustments, at once social and private, that exact the essential while apparently requiring the insignificant. The fashioning of the socially legible body amounts in effect to a coordination of bodily and economic practices in terms of a specific social physiognomy.

The realist text is, we have seen, replete with instances of such a social physiognomy. It is visible, for example, on the opening page of *The American,* in the "profound enjoyment of [Newman's] posture," "head thrown back and legs outstretched," that denotes the "serene possession" of the commercial person: "his physiognomy would have sufficiently indicated that he was a shrewd and capable fellow" (17). Or, to take another example from the following page of this story, a story in which looking is everywhere linked, as we have seen, to acquisition, consumerism, and bodily and economic reproductions: "it was our friend's eye that chiefly told his story." The paradoxical look readable in that eye constitutes, for both James and Marx, the paradoxical disposition of the capitalist: "It was full of contradictory suggestions. . . . Frigid yet friendly, frank and yet cautious, shrewd yet credulous, positive yet sceptical, confident yet shy, extremely intelligent and extremely good-humoured, there was something vaguely defiant in its concessions, and something reassuring in its reserve" (18–19).[40] The very excessiveness of James's reading of the businessman's eye foregrounds the extraordinary legibility of the socially informed body.

In this view, the discrepancies between meaning and materiality, and between structure and self, appear somewhat differently. If realism relies on such a social physiognomy, we have also seen that the novel points to a *discrepancy* between the subject's will and the structure he inhabits, points to a certain *dis*articulation of private dispositions and something in life stronger than his own will. Perhaps it is now possible, however, to consider this contradiction as something more than an instance of realism's double logic, or even as an embodiment of the contradictory imperatives of the contractual self. It may be possible to consider how these contradictions and differences are adjusted and coordinated in the novel, how these very conflicts and contradictions are at once solicited by the novel and tactically deployed and "managed." That is, it may be possible to discover, in this solicitation and management of a "logic" of difference and contradiction, the logistics by which a politics of representation operates and in which the social effect of realism inheres.

The duty of the subject of realism is to fashion a character that corresponds to its representations (the duty of resembling oneself). The duty of a certain realism is to fashion a subject who corresponds to, exemplifies, and embodies the social meanings that, completing the tautology, inform him. There is thus a social work immanent in the realist imperative of the social legibility of character: It is, on one level, the constant adjustment of subject and structure and, on another, the perpetual coordination of bodies and meanings, content and form, that the realist novel enacts. The realist criteria of legible social types, consistency of character, and deterministic and linear narrative progress function to secure at once the intelligibility and supervision of character and event.[41]

But the realist text is not merely *about* the fashioning of socially informed bodies; the novel also *underwrites* such a fashioning. The socially informed body of the character of realism may appear as a second nature, or indeed as nature itself – as the embodied form of "the physical capital which the owner does nothing to 'keep up.'" The achievement of such an "almost ideal completeness" is something of an advertisement for an ideally complete realism. But it is just the too perfect completeness of the "variously embodied human nature" (60) James portrays in *The American* that indicates a certain "romantic" resistance to realism and to the relations that constitute it. The realist body is never quite so well informed, never quite so autonomously complete and unrelated; the realist body is always "to be completed."

For the realist novel there is no end to the work of "keeping up"; no end to the work of disclosing and accounting for the discrepancies between what things and persons look like and what they "are"; no end to the work of "adjusting" subjects and structures, coordinating local and everyday practices and dispositions and the "official" or formal principles of power and meaning (laws, rules, ruling representations) in relation to, and against which, these practices function.[42] And if these practices are never quite faithful to their principles, the realist text capitalizes on precisely this discrepancy, advertising the differences between persons and things, will and structure, content and form even as it reinforces and extends the links and exchanges between them. There is always physical capital to be made, and made, as both novelists and capitalists in the American paper system are well aware, out of little pieces of paper. And the consumer of the realist text reenacts – embodies – these adjustments and exchanges as with the turning of a page.

NOTES

1. Harriet Beecher Stowe, *Uncle Tom's Cabin* (Harmondsworth: Penguin Books, 1981), pp. 480–1. Subsequent references are to this edition and are cited parenthetically by page number in the text.
2. Charlotte Perkins Gilman, "The Yellow Wallpaper," in *Charlotte Perkins Gilman Reader* (New York: Pantheon Books, 1980), pp. 7–8.
3. Henry James, *The American,* ed. James W. Tuttleton (New York: Norton, 1978), p. 303. Subsequent references to the novel and preface are to this edition, which follows the London Macmillan edition of 1879, and are cited parenthetically by page number in the text.
4. In his recent *The Bourgeois and the Bibelot* (New Brunswick, N.J.: Rutgers University Press, 1984), Remy G. Saisselin discusses the "bibelotization" of both art and women in the bourgeois consumerist aesthetic. He points as well to the close "parallels between museums and department stores" in this culture of consumption (pp. 33–49). Newman's viewing of the stream of girls through the huge wall of plate-glass clearly invokes the aesthetics of the department store, which centrally relies on the display of objects through the recent innovation of the glass wall; and Claire is, of course, both the best article in the market and an *objet d'art* for Newman. James's depiction of consumerism anticipates the metaphysics of shopping most powerfully articulated in Zola's *Au Bonheur des dames* (1883) and Dreiser's *Sister Carrie* (1900). Saisselin further notes that "the flaneur might escape the lure of consumer goods merely by stepping from the Magasin du Louvre into the Musée du Louvre, to stroll, gaze, and lounge. Yet even here he might be attracted by objects – objects beyond his desire only because they could not be purchased" (41). Newman's consumption of copies goes this distinction one better. "I have just bought a picture," he tells Tristram. " 'Bought a picture?' said Mr. Tristram, looking vaguely round at the walls [of the Musée du Louvre]. 'Why, do they sell them?' " (27). I will discuss the scene

of the museum and of copying in a moment; my concern, however, is less with an economy of consumption – the world as department store – than with its ties to a more general economy of persons and things. In addition to Saisselin, see Jean-Christophe Agnew's "The Consuming Vision of Henry James" in *The Culture of Consumption: Critical Essays in American History, 1880–1980,* ed. Richard Wightman Fox and T. J. Jackson Lears (New York: Pantheon Books, 1983), pp. 67–100; and Michael B. Miller, *The Bon Marché: Bourgeois Culture and the Department Store, 1869–1920* (Princeton: Princeton University Press, 1981).

5. James's review (which appeared in *The Nation* 20 [May 6, 1875]: 318–19) is reprinted in the Norton Critical Edition of *The American,* pp. 324–6. In *Notes on Paris,* Taine observes that "Women and works of art are related creatures. . . . What is really wanted of them is possession or exhibition." *Notes sur Paris* (Paris: Hachette, 1901), p. 307.

6. Edward Bellamy, *Looking Backward, 2000–1887* (Cambridge, Mass.: Harvard University Press, 1967), p. 141.

7. David M. Potter, *People of Plenty: Economic Abundance and the American Character* (Chicago: University of Chicago Press, 1954), pp. 118–19. On the history and effects of American mass production and mechanical reproduction, see *Yankee Enterprise: The Rise of the American System of Manufactures,* ed. Otto Mayr and Robert C. Post (Washington, D.C.: Smithsonian Institution Press, 1981), especially the essays by Alfred D. Chandler and Neil Harris. It is worth noting that the commerce in copies also directly affected not only the economics of book publishing in the later nineteenth century but also the status of the author as owner and producer of his work. On the right to copy and attempts to regulate it, see Walter L. Pforzheimer's informative "Historical Perspective on Copyright Law and Fair Use" in *Reprography and Copyright Law,* ed. Lowell H. Lattery and George P. Bush (Washington, D.C.: American Institute of Biological Sciences, 1964), pp. 18–35. See also Christopher P. Wilson, *The Labor of Words: Literary Professionalism in the Progressive Era* (Athens: University of Georgia Press, 1985), esp. chap. 3; and my *Henry James and the Art of Power* (Ithaca, N.Y.: Cornell University Press, 1984), pp. 162–6.

8. Richard Poirier provides a related but ultimately alternative account of the type in his richly perceptive treatment of *The American* in *The Comic Sense of Henry James: A Study of the Early Novels* (New York: Oxford University Press, 1960), pp. 44–94. On the Jamesian type, see also William Veeder, *Henry James – The Lessons of the Master: Popular*

Fiction and Personal Style in the Nineteenth Century (Chicago: University of Chicago Press, 1975), pp. 106–83.

9. Early readers of the novel, more recent critics, and James himself commented on the underdetermined logic of the novel's breaking off of relations; but, if it is not hard to "psychologize" this desire for an unrelated state, my concern here is with the remarkable configuration of sexual, economic, and representational interests solicited by the Jamesian problem of "relation" and with the ways in which this configuration *constitutes* what counts as a person in the Jamesian text. The Norton Critical Edition conveniently collects much of the relevant material; see for instance, in addition to the preface, James's letters to William Dean Howells, October 24, 1876, and March 30, 1877 (pp. 343–4, 348–9); the reviews in *The Nation*, May 31, 1877 (pp. 391–2) and in *The Galaxy*, July 1877 (pp. 394–7). See also Leon Edel, *Henry James: The Conquest of London, 1870–1881* (Philadelphia: Lippincott, 1962), pp. 248–60.

10. Henry James, *Hawthorne* (1879; reprint Ithaca, N.Y.: Cornell University Press, 1966), pp. 99–105.

11. Nathaniel Hawthorne, *The House of the Seven Gables*, ed. Seymour L. Gross (New York: Norton, 1967), pp. 151–2. Subsequent references are to this edition and are cited parenthetically by page number in the text.

12. Hawthorne here provides a sort of barnyard version of the "transcendental" correspondence between bodies or material things and the meanings they embody. I will address the realist rewriting of such a correspondence in what follows. On embodiment in Hawthorne, see Sharon Cameron's provocative *The Corporeal Self: Allegories of the Body in Melville and Hawthorne* (Baltimore: Johns Hopkins University Press, 1981), pp. 77–157. On heredity, biology, and the body in the nineteenth-century novel, see Gillian Beer, *Darwin's Plots: Evolutionary Narrative in Darwin, George Eliot and Nineteenth-Century Fiction* (London: Ark, 1983); Peter Morton, *The Vital Science: Biology and the Literary Imagination, 1860–1900* (London: Allen & Unwin, 1984). My account of embodiment is also indebted to Elaine Scarry, *The Body in Pain: The Making and Unmaking of the World* (New York: Oxford University Press, 1985).

13. Hawthorne's animistic domestic economy, like Stowe's, disavows the impersonality of things. "Phoebe, and the fire that boiled in the teakettle," for instance, "were equally bright, cheerful, and efficient, in their respective offices" (p. 76); Rachel Halliday "put a spirit into the food and drink she offered" and domestic objects "arrange" *them-*

selves as if "in obedience to a few gentle whispers" (pp. 217–23). "The fact was, it was, after all, the THING that I hated" (p. 342), St. Clare declares, and what St. Clare hates is not merely the fact of slavery but the fact of the impersonal THING itself. Crucially, the protest against turning persons into things (a critique of reification) involves also an insistence on turning things into persons (an imperative of personification). Such an emphasis is not, of course, limited to the domestic and sentimental novel or treatise. Oliver Wendell Holmes, for example, in the first lecture of *The Common Law* (1880; Boston: Little, Brown, 1963), focuses on the persistence in liability and property law of the "metaphysical confusion" that involves a "personification of inanimate nature" (pp. 30, 12). I address some further implications of this imperative of personification in the final section.

14. On the sexualization of the nineteenth-century family, see Carroll Smith-Rosenberg, *Disorderly Conduct: Visions of Gender in Victorian America* (New York: Knopf, 1985); Michel Foucault, *The History of Sexuality*, Vol. 1, trans. Robert Hurley (New York: Pantheon Books, 1978).

15. Albert O. Hirschman comments on the persistent noncommercial and specifically sexual meanings of "commerce" in *The Passions and the Interests: Political Arguments for Capitalism before Its Triumph* (Princeton, N.J.: Princeton University Press, 1977), pp. 61–3. Note also the terms of John Dewey's euphoric description of commerce in his "Pragmatic America" (1922): "Commerce itself, let us dare to say it, is a noble thing. It is intercourse, exchange, communication, distribution, sharing of what is otherwise secluded and private." *Pragmatism and American Culture*, ed. Gail Kennedy (Heath, 1950), p. 59.

16. It is impossible here to provide an extended account of Hawthorne's novel. But I suggest that whereas in *The American* the romance is set in opposition to the social, in Hawthorne's work the romance is set in opposition to the very *category* of the "social." On the invention of the "social sector" in the nineteenth century, see Raymond Williams, *Culture and Society, 1780–1950* (New York: Columbia University Press, 1958), and Jacques Donzelot, *The Policing of Families*, trans. Robert Hurley (New York: Pantheon Books, 1979), pp. xxvi, 88–90.

17. Leo Bersani, "The Jamesian Lie," *A Future for Astyanax* (Boston: Little, Brown, 1976), p. 135.

18. James's highly abstract treatment of models of marriage and family in the novel does not simply oppose Newman's new state of the family to the hereditary nobility of the Bellegarde's (a succession of portraits

163

in which Claire's "face was a larger and freer copy" of her mother's [120] and Urbain "the old woman at second-hand" [123]) but also involves the Babcock episode as a kind of homosocial trial marriage. As Newman puts it in his letter to Mrs. Tristram, "The nearest approach to [Claire] was a Unitarian minister from Boston, who very soon demanded a separation, for incompatibility of temper" (76).

19. Thomas L. Haskell, "Capitalism and the Origins of the Humanitarian Sensibility, Part 2," *The American Historical Review* 90, no. 2 (June 1985): 551.

20. Ibid., 553. On the relations of marriage, promise keeping, and contract in nineteenth-century America, see Michael Grossberg, *Governing the Hearth: Law and the Family in Nineteenth-Century America* (Chapel Hill: University of North Carolina Press, 1985), pp. 17–63. On contractualism generally, see P. S. Atiyah, *The Rise and Fall of Freedom of Contract* (London, 1979); Morton J. Horwitz, *The Transformation of American Law* (Cambridge, Mass.: Harvard University Press, 1977).

21. Friedrich Nietzsche, *On the Genealogy of Morals* (New York: Vintage Books, 1969), pp. 57–8; cited by Haskell, "Capitalism and the Origins of the Humanitarian Sensibility, Part 2," 551–2.

22. William James, *The Principles of Psychology,* Vol. 1 (1890; reprint of the first edition, New York: Dover, 1950), pp. 338–40. On the "possessive individual," see C. B. Macpherson, *The Political Theory of Possessive Individualism: Hobbes to Locke* (Oxford: Clarendon Press, 1962), and Magali Sarfatti Larson, *The Rise of Professionalism: A Sociological Analysis* (Berkeley and Los Angeles: University of California Press, 1977), pp. 222–5.

23. See, for instance, pp. 17, 89, 188, 190. I discuss the larger significance of physiognomy in the realist novel in the final section.

24. On the paper system, see Irwin Unger, *The Greenback Era: A Social and Political History of American Finance, 1865–1879* (Princeton, N.J.: Princeton University Press, 1967); Richard Hofstadter, "Free Silver and the Mind of 'Coin' Harvey," in *The Paranoid Style in American Politics and Other Essays* (Chicago: University of Chicago Press, 1979), pp. 238–315; Walter T. K. Nugent, *Money and American Society, 1865–1880* (New York: Free Press, 1968). As Nugent observes in *The Money Question During Reconstruction* (New York: Norton, 1967), "No one realized in 1865, but money was destined to become the chief perennial issue in national politics for over thirty years. . . . Its peculiar dimensions were established in almost all important ways during the Reconstruction years, from 1867 to 1879" (pp. 21–2).

25. Marc Shell, "The Gold Bug," *Genre* 13, no. 1 (Spring 1980): 18.

26. George Eliot, *Middlemarch* (Harmondsworth: Penguin Books, 1965), p. 173.

27. This tension also appears in the novel in terms of a perplexity about "whether to attribute" acts and expressions "to habit or to intention, to art or to nature" (115). The problematic relation between act and determining structure, between freedom and predictability or typicality, appears as well, in the period, as a problem of statistical probability. Newman, James notes, "was fond of statistics; he liked to know how things were done" (55). As Emerson noted early on, "the new science of Statistics" (along with the new sciences of physiognomy and heredity) provides an exemplary instance of "the stealthy power of other laws which act on us daily . . . organization tyrannizing over character." Statistical analysis, as Emerson indicates, posits "a rule that the most casual and extraordinary events . . . become matter of fixed calculation." "Fate" (1852) in *Selections from Ralph Waldo Emerson*, ed. Stephen E. Whicher (Boston: Houghton Mifflin, 1957), pp. 337, 333. On statistics and their social application, see Lorraine J. Daston, "Rational Individuals *Versus* Laws of Society: From Probability to Statistics," in *Probability Since 1800: Interdisciplinary Studies of Scientific Development* (Bielefeld, 1983), pp. 7–26; and my "Statistical Persons," in *Bodies and Machines* (Methuen, forthcoming).

28. Thomas L. Haskell, "Capitalism and the Origins of the Humanitarian Sensibility, Part 1," *The American Historical Review* 90, no. 2 (April 1985): 341–53. On classical and modern conceptionalizations of the category of "interest," see Patricia Springborg, *The Problem of Human Needs and the Critique of Civilization* (London: Allen & Unwin, 1981).

29. Foucault's remark in a personal communication is cited in Hubert L. Dreyfus and Paul Rabinow, *Michel Foucault: Beyond Structuralism and Hermeneutics* (Chicago: University of Chicago Press, 1982), p. 187; Pierre Bourdieu, *Outline of a Theory of Practice*, trans. Richard Nice (Cambridge: Cambridge University Press, 1977), p. 79. Although I have abstracted these statements in order to exemplify the recalcitrant and rival positions on the problem of subject and structure I am concerned with here, these remarks scarcely represent the significant reconceptualizations of the problem in the work of Foucault and Bourdieu.

30. Haskell, "Capitalism and the Origins of the Humanitarian Sensibility, Part 1," 347, 343.

31. Thorstein Veblen, *The Theory of the Leisure Class* (1899; New York: New American Library, 1953), pp. 184, 187, 188, 186.

32. I am thinking particularly about recent accounts of "structural causality" (Althusser), "structural intentionality" (Derrida), "objective intention" (Bourdieu), and also accounts of the irreducibility of structure and intention (de Man). See, for instance, Louis Althusser, *For Marx*, trans. Ben Brewster (London: New Left Books, 1977); Jacques Derrida, "Limited Inc," *Glyph 2: Johns Hopkins Textual Studies* (Baltimore: Johns Hopkins University Press, 1977), pp. 192–217; Bourdieu, *Outline of a Theory of Practice*, pp. 78–81; Paul de Man, "The Purloined Ribbon," *Glyph 1: Johns Hopkins Textual Studies* (Baltimore: Johns Hopkins University Press, 1977). Vincent Descombes provides an informed history of the shifting relations of subject and structure in *Modern French Philosophy*, trans. L. Scott-Fox and J. M. Harding (Cambridge: Cambridge University Press, 1980).

33. See Karl Polanyi, *Primitive, Archaic, and Modern Economics*, ed. George Dalton (New York: Doubleday, 1968) and *The Great Transformation* (New York: Holt, Rinehart, 1944); Bourdieu, *Outline of a Theory of Practice*, pp. 183–97.

34. Haskell, "Capitalism and the Origins of the Humanitarian Sensibility, Part 2," 547.

35. Walter Benn Michaels, "The Gold Standard and the Logic of Naturalism," *Representations* 9 (Winter 1985): 105–32. My references here are to an expanded version of this essay that will appear in Michaels's *The Gold Standard and the Logic of Naturalism* (University of California Press, forthcoming in 1987). Michaels's conclusion centers on the remark made by Foucault previously quoted. I am grateful to Walter Michaels for permission to quote from this piece.

36. See, for instance, Michaels and Steven Knapp, "Against Theory," *Critical Inquiry* 8, no. 4 (Summer 1982): 723–42. Whereas "Against Theory" argues for the inseparability of meaning and intention ("Meaning is just another name for expressed intention"), the double logic of "The Gold Standard" involves an irreducible distinction between intention and meaning and between "material and identity," and the interdependent and interconvertible oppositions between these terms govern Michaels's account. My point is that such a double logic closely resembles precisely the "radical formalism" (particularly the work of Paul de Man) that Michaels's argument against theory targets. Despite and alongside these differences, however, my emphases at this point and elsewhere are directly indebted to Michaels's

treatments of American literature and economics and also to conversations about the topics I address.

37. In "Truth and Power," Michel Foucault argues that "neither the dialectic, as a logic of contradictions, nor semiotics, as the structure of communication, can account for the intrinsic intelligibility of conflicts." *Power/Knowledge: Selected Interviews and Other Writings, 1972–1977,* ed. Colin Gordon (New York: Pantheon Books), p. 114. This "intrinsic intelligibility" of events and conflicts is what I am describing here as a social logistics.

38. "The Naturalist Machine," *Sex, Politics, and Science in the Nineteenth-Century Novel: Selected Papers from the English Institute, 1983–1984,* ed. Ruth Bernard Yeazell (Baltimore: Johns Hopkins University Press, 1985), pp. 116–47.

39. Bourdieu, *Outline of a Theory of Practice,* p. 124.

40. The capitalist, according to Marx, must "have fine hearing and a thick skin; must be simultaneously cautious and venturesome, a swashbuckler and a calculator, careless and prudent. He must, in fine, develop all the qualities of an experienced man of business." Marx as quoted in Matthew Josephson, *The Robber Barons: The Great American Capitalists, 1861–1901* (New York: Harcourt, Brace, 1934), p. 192.

41. "*The Princess Casamassima:* Realism and the Fantasy of Surveillance," *Nineteenth-Century Fiction* 35, no. 4 (March 1981): 506–34.

42. This work of adjustment and coordination is perhaps most evident in the communications elaborated between formal, juridical, and economic determinations of the subject (the theory and logic of contract) and the minute and everyday policies of bodies (the logistics of the realist body). See, for instance, Michel Foucault, *Discipline and Punish: The Birth of the Prison,* trans. Alan Sheridan (New York: Pantheon, 1977), pp. 222–3, 303–5. The links, relays, and communications progressively set in place between juridical and economic principles, on the one side, and small, everyday physical mechanisms and corporeal dispositions, on the other, must finally be understood, I think, in terms of what we might call the realist project of accounting for persons – the project of accounting for the "discovery" that a person is something that can be made. This project and its implications are further discussed in my *Bodies and Machines* (Methuen, forthcoming), in which a version of the present essay will appear.

Notes on Contributors

Martha Banta has recently published *Imaging American Women: Idea and Ideals in Cultural History*. She is Professor of English at the University of California, Los Angeles.

Peter Brooks is Tripp Professor of Humanities at Yale University. His latest book is *Reading for the Plot*.

Carolyn Porter, Associate Professor of English at the University of California, Berkeley, has published *Seeing and Being: The Plight of the Participant Observer in Emerson, James, Adams, and Faulkner*.

John Carlos Rowe is Professor of English at the University of California, Irvine. His most recent books are *The Theoretical Dimensions of Henry James* and *At Emerson's Tomb: The Politics of American Modernism*.

Mark Seltzer, author of *Henry James and the Art of Power*, is Assistant Professor of English at Cornell University.

Selected Bibliography

Four of the essayists in this collection refer to the 1879 edition of *The American* published by Macmillan in London and one to the New York edition brought out by Osgood in 1877, but all five use the pagination provided by the Norton Critical Edition of 1978, edited by James P. Tuttleton, which reprints the 1879 text. The Introduction discusses the various reasons why readers over the years have shown their liking for one or the other of these "original" versions. (The Macmillan text is considered to be the one "authorized" by James after he made minor corrections upon the Osgood text.) *The American* as extensively revised by James for Scribner's New York Edition, published in 1907, continues to have its champions as *the* text of preference and always enters into any extended consideration of the novel.

The books and articles concerning Henry James's writing career number in the hundreds; many touch upon *The American*. The following list suggests some useful essay-length treatments of James's novel. The footnotes to the essays contained in this volume yield further references to writings on *The American*.

Antush, John V. "The 'Much Finer Complexity' of History in *The American*," *Journal of American Studies* 6 (1972):85–95.

Banta, Martha. "Rebirth and Revenge: The Endings of *Huckleberry Finn* and *The American*," *Modern Fiction Studies* 15 (Summer 1969):191–207.

Blasing, Mutlu. "Double Focus in *The American*," *Nineteenth Century Fiction* 28 (1973):74–84.

Brooks, Cleanth. "The American Innocence," *Shenandoah* 16 (1964):21–37.

Butterfield, R. W. "*The American*," in *The Air of Reality: New Essays on Henry James*, ed. John Goode. London: Methuen, 1972.

Cargill, Oscar. "The First International Novel," *PMLA* 73 (1958):418–25.

Clair, John A. "*The American*: A Reinterpretation," *PMLA* 74 (1959):613–18.

Gargano, James W. "Foreshadowing in *The American,*" *Modern Language Notes* 74 (1959):600–1.

Goldsmith, Arnold L. "Henry James's Reconciliation of Free Will and Fatalism," *Nineteenth-Century Fiction* 13 (1958):109–26.

Hays, H. R. "The Limitations of Christopher Newman," in *Henry James: The American,* ed. Gerald Willen. New York: Thomas Y. Crowell, 1972.

Hoffman, Frederick J. "Freedom and Conscious Form: Henry James and the American Self," *Virginia Quarterly Review* 37 (1961):269–85.

Horowitz, Floyd R. "The Christian Time Sequence in Henry James's *The American,*" *CLA Journal* 9 (1966):234–45.

Knox, George. "Romance and Fable in James's *The American,*" *Anglia* 83 (1965):308–23.

Lerner, Daniel. "The Influence of Turgenev on Henry James," *Slavonic Review* 20 (1941):28–54.

Reynolds, Larry. "Henry James's New Christopher Newman," *Studies in the Novel* 5 (Winter 1973):457–68.

Schulz, Max F. "The Bellegardes' Feud with Christopher Newman: A Study of Henry James's Revision of *The American,*" *American Literature* 27 (1955):42–55.

Secor, Robert. "Christopher Newman: How Innocent Is James's American?" *Studies in American Fiction* 1 (1973):141–53.

Stafford, William T. "The Ending of Henry James's *The American:* A Defense of the Early Version," *Nineteenth-Century Fiction* 18 (1963):86–89.

Tick, Stanley. "Henry James's *The American:* Voyons," *Studies in the Novel* (North Texas State University) 2 (1970):276–91.

Traschen, Isadore. "An American in Paris," *American Literature* 26 (1954):67–77.

"James's Revisions of the Love Affair in *The American,*" *New England Quarterly* 29 (1956):43–62.

Tuttleton, James W. "Henry James: The Superstitious Valuation of Europe," from *The Novel of Manners in America* (New York: W. W. Norton, 1974), pp. 48–85.

Van Der Beets, Richard. "A Note on Henry James's Western Barbarian," *Western Humanities Review* 17 (1963):175–8.

Vanderbilt, Kermit. "James, Fitzgerald, and the American Self-Image," *Massachusetts Review* 6 (1965):289–304.

Watkins, Floyd C. "Christopher Newman's Final Instinct," *Nineteenth-Century Fiction* 12 (1957):85–8.

Zeitlow, Edward R. "A Flaw in The American," *CLA Journal* 9 (1966):246–54.

172

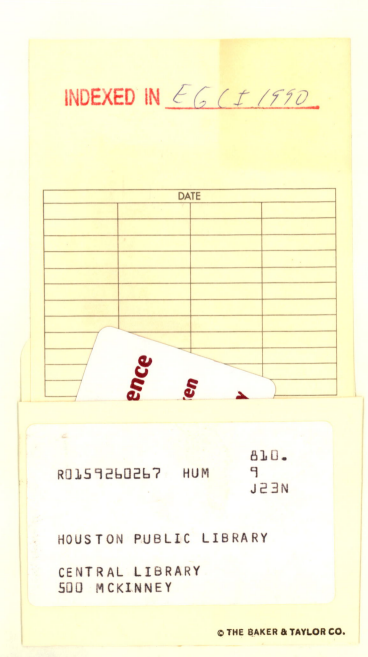